FOUND

ALSO BY TATUM O'NEAL
A Paper Life

FOUND

A Daughter's Journey Home

TATUM O'NEAL
with Hilary Liftin

WILLIAM MORROW
An Imprint of HarperCollinsPublishers

FOUND. Copyright © 2011 by Tatum O'Neal. All rights reserved. Printed in the United States of America. No part of this book may be used or reproduced in any manner whatsoever without written permission except in the case of brief quotations embodied in critical articles and reviews. For information address HarperCollins Publishers, 10 East 53rd Street, New York, NY 10022.

HarperCollins books may be purchased for educational, business, or sales promotional use. For information please write: Special Markets Department, HarperCollins Publishers, 10 East 53rd Street, New York, NY 10022.

FIRST EDITION

Designed by Lisa Stokes

Library of Congress Cataloging-in-Publication Data has been applied for.

ISBN 978-0-06-206656-5

11 12 13 14 15   OV/QGF   10 9 8 7 6 5 4 3 2 1

To my children, Kevin, Sean, and Emily—
The true loves of my life and the shining stars of my story.
And to my dear friend Perry Moore—
You taught me to be a more loving and compassionate
person and I will miss you dearly.
You were a hero.

CONTENTS

INTRODUCTION   1

PART I: Fractures   15

CHAPTER ONE   Outside and In   17

CHAPTER TWO   Home Again   25

CHAPTER THREE   Father and Son   31

CHAPTER FOUR   Is That You?   37

CHAPTER FIVE   Reconciliation   46

CHAPTER SIX   The New O'Neals   56

CHAPTER SEVEN   The Storm After the Calm   65

CHAPTER EIGHT   Down to the Wire   70

CHAPTER NINE   Cold Feet   77

CHAPTER TEN   How Can You Do This to Me?   84

CHAPTER ELEVEN   Cause and Effect   89

CHAPTER TWELVE   Two Nights   95

CHAPTER THIRTEEN   On Again   104

CHAPTER FOURTEEN   Beautiful Creatures   109

CHAPTER FIFTEEN | Wild-goose Chase | 117

PART II: REGRET AND HOPE | 123
CHAPTER SIXTEEN | The Man Behind the Curtain | 125
CHAPTER SEVENTEEN | Better Late Than Never | 129
CHAPTER EIGHTEEN | Regret | 136
CHAPTER NINETEEN | An Unrepentant Ghost | 144
CHAPTER TWENTY | Disconnect | 148
CHAPTER TWENTY-ONE | The New Generation | 157
CHAPTER TWENTY-TWO | Ryan's Eyes | 162

PART III: GRACE | 171
CHAPTER TWENTY-THREE | Everything's Perfect | 173
CHAPTER TWENTY-FOUR | My Own | 181
CHAPTER TWENTY-FIVE | Christmas Rain Date | 186
AFTERWORD | Found | 193

ACKNOWLEDGMENTS | 203

My dream is to remember to laugh at myself when I've been a fool . . . and to learn from it, and then let it go.

—*My mother, Joanna Moore (1934–1997)*

FOUND

INTRODUCTION

IT WAS SUNDAY evening, June 2, 2008. My cell phone rang, its familiar ring, as if everything were okay. The same old ring, as if it were still six hours ago, or yesterday, or last week, any time in the past, when this wasn't happening, and the day was sorting itself out the way days always did, with to-dos and phone calls and all the mundanities that add up to a normal life. A cheerful, oblivious ring. Who was calling at this terrible juncture? Was it someone who could help? A friend or ally with a sixth sense for when I was in trouble? Or was it just some random caller, barging innocently into this moment like a bystander strolling onto a movie set? I leaned over as far as I could to see the phone's display.

Emily.

I sank back into my seat, my heart collapsing in on itself.

My sixteen-year-old daughter, Emily, was calling, and I couldn't answer. I was breaking my promise to her, and we both knew what that meant.

I WAS AND continue to be an imperfect mother. My children, like the children of anyone who suffers from addiction, have had to bear the burden of premature knowledge and fear. But my love for them is so strong it can border on obsessive. Always, no matter how I struggled with my own problems, I tried to protect them. I tried to be their mother. I tried to let them be children. But there was a period of time, in the 1990s and the early 2000s, when my sobriety was in flux. My children's connection to me, the connection that makes children feel like nothing can go wrong in the world, was threatened. During that time, if I was using drugs, I could and would go missing while the kids were at John's house. Consequently, I would be unreachable by phone. My phone battery, left uncharged, would die. Or my voice mail would fill up. Or I'd turn the phone off.

One day in 2003, when I was in much better shape, Emily, who was eleven at the time, brought up the matter of reaching me by phone. We were lying in my bed together, her long brown hair fanned out across the pillow. Without looking directly at me, she said, "When you don't answer your phone, I don't know where you are." She didn't elaborate, but I felt the concern in her tone. She was already mature for her age. She had known from the time she was little to worry if Mom was in the bathroom for too long, to worry if I didn't answer the phone or return her calls promptly.

I was a daughter, too. I was a daughter who needed her mother to be sober. I never got that gift. My mother was a kind, loving woman, my angel, and I have long understood and forgiven her failings, but the truth of the matter is that she never got sober, and I never saw her try. But I did not want that destiny. Not for me, and not with kids.

With every fiber of my being, I wanted my children's experience to be completely different from mine. They were all academic successes—from a mother who didn't finish high school—but that wasn't enough. I wanted to be honest with them and to be sober for them. And I wanted to preserve their childhoods. A kid shouldn't be worrying about her mother. She should be wondering what's for dinner, or whether she has the right outfit for the school dance. My addiction was my own problem. My own issue. My own cross to bear. Mine alone. I was bearing it as best I could. I was fighting, and even though my track record was bad, I planned on winning. I was sorry for every point at which my struggles entered my children's lives.

Stroking Emily's hair, I told her I would always answer the phone when she called. I would never turn it off. There would always be a line open. *I'll always have the phone on for you* meant *I'll always stay sober for you.* That was our deal.

I wish it were that simple. God, do I ever.

NOW, FIVE YEARS later, I was missing Emily's call for the first time since I'd made that promise. I couldn't answer Emily's call, and I knew that she would assume the worst. Rightly so. I had just been arrested for trying to buy crack on a street corner on the Lower East Side of Manhattan. I was in a police station, being booked.

There was a turnstile at the entrance to the jail. Before I went through, someone took my watch, my wallet, and my phone, and put them in a basket. My phone started ringing as they plucked it out of my hand, an audible reminder of my failure. "No!" I wailed, "I've got to get it!" But it was too late. This was jail, baby. I had lost everything.

THIS WASN'T SUPPOSED to happen. I was supposed to be all better. In the past six years of stability, I'd written a memoir called *A Paper Life*. Writing a book like that was supposed to be cathartic. Ostensibly, if I took all of the suffering and trauma of my childhood and all of the missteps and mistakes of my adulthood and transformed them into little black marks on white pages, then I could literally "close the book" on the past, put it up on a shelf next to my unread copy of *The Great Gatsby*, and never think about it again. Publishing the book was supposed to symbolize the end of one life and the beginning of another. It was supposed to mean that from then on I was clean, healed, and finally free.

Unfortunately, my book contract did not guarantee these results. As it turned out, writing the book wasn't remotely healing. Not at first, anyway. I wrote *A Paper Life* in 2004, after a terrible run in Los Angeles because of which I had lost my kids to my ex-husband. My soul and spirit just weren't strong or sober enough to put it all on paper and move on. Opening up about the things that had happened to me as a child didn't erase the past or transform it to a heartwarming tale of triumph over adversity. That would have been swell. Instead, writing the book was painful. When I summoned the past, it rose to the surface like embedded shrapnel, exiting more slowly than it entered, but still sharp, twisted, and destructive. So much for catharsis.

In *A Paper Life*, I talked about a childhood in which, under the care of a mother who, in spite of her big heart, was utterly lost to drugs and her own tragedy, my younger brother Griffin and I were left to survive as best we could, living in a run-down ranch in Reseda, California, as little barefoot street urchins whose daily activities included starting fires, playing with knives, and jumping off roof-tops. My mother had bought the ranch with the misguided notion that she would save young kids, but it became an unsafe place, har-boring teenage runaways and juvenile delinquents. There were drugs and there was criminal activity. My mother had a sixteen-year-old boyfriend, who beat us with switches cut from the fig tree. We were locked in the garage for so long that we ate dog food to quell our hunger. We were unsupervised and wild. My father, Ryan O'Neal, the star of *Love Story,* that golden boy from the big screen, swept in, rescued me, put me in the movie *Paper Moon,* and I was saved. I won a Best Supporting Actress Oscar for *Paper Moon.* I was eight years old when we started filming, and I was nine when I took home my statuette, which made me the youngest Academy Award win-ner in history. For a while, I was my father's favorite escort around A-list Hollywood. He was brilliantly funny and handsome, and we had a very special bond. But my relief and happiness were short-lived. When I was fifteen and so sadly awkward, Ryan fell in love with beauty Farrah Fawcett and moved to her home in Beverly Hills, leaving me and Griffin alone in his Malibu house to figure out why we had been abandoned by the parent who was supposed to be our savior.

In *A Paper Life,* I talked about my marriage to tennis player John McEnroe, during which we quickly had three children, Kevin, Sean, and Emily, in that order. John eventually lost his number-one rank-ing, and our marriage crumbled under the weight of his disappointment and my lifetime of trauma. I'd kept my demons at bay during my marriage by running every day, dieting, watching tennis, taking care of the children, and focusing so intently on the external world that I didn't have to face my internal pain and the disease that was inextricably bound to it. They say that addiction, left untreated, does push-ups, getting bigger and stronger while it waits for you to come back and get sucked into it again.

John McEnroe (he was always "John McEnroe" to me—you know you've got trouble when you think of your own husband by his full tennis champion name) and I separated, then divorced, and he had the kids for two out of every four weeks. I wrote how in their absence my whole world crashed down. A shell of myself, I faced the darkness that had been with me as long as I could remember. I met a boy who introduced me to heroin, which promised to take away the pain, and it was a fast descent from there.

A Paper Life chronicled a lifelong struggle, and when the press got their hands on it, they looked to me for the lesson learned. Every memoir of trauma and abuse is supposed to have a fairy-tale ending, or, at the very least, an "everything's okay now" ending. I was interviewed by Oprah, Stone Phillips, Katie Couric, and others. What had I gained from this sad, lost childhood? What was the point of the suffering? Where was the triumph over adversity? When was my "aha" moment? I could feel them searching for something I hadn't begun to imagine. The deeper they probed for the requisite epiphany, the more that emerging shrapnel poked brutally at the surface tissue. I felt so raw, so exposed. I didn't have what they were looking for. I didn't have the distance from my life and my disease to step back and see what the message was. I was still too broken.

Nonetheless, after *A Paper Life* came out in October 2004, it appeared to me, my friends and family, and the rest of the world that I was out of the woods. We were all convinced. The book did well. The bitter, heart-wrenching custody battles that had lasted for eight years came to a close, thank God. I had been passing my court-mandated urine tests for years without protest or incident. The only blip on the media radar happened in 2003. I had a drink with a woman, and although I'm not gay—what can I say? We made out in a restaurant, and the next morning the cover of the *New York Post* screamed, "Tatum O'Neal's Sapphic Lesbian Love Spree." John went to court to have my visitation rights revoked, but hallelujah for Judge Silverman! She turned him down.

So, unthwarted by my moment of playing for the other team, I had my children back. My family was stable. I had a long-term boyfriend, an architect named Ron Castellano. I regularly met with my 12-step support group to manage my addiction. Even my acting career was back on track. I had a part on the TV series *Rescue Me*, starring Denis Leary.

And yet, there was my cell phone, the urgent vibrations of its ring making it quiver in the plastic basket on the desk of the police station like a hesitant, terrified mouse.

THE ARREST HAPPENED on a Sunday at dusk. At the time, I was living in a gorgeous building on the Lower East Side of Manhattan, on East Broadway and Essex. I knew that there was a lot of drug activity around, though I'd never copped drugs in this neighborhood before (and never would again). I was wearing a little T-shirt and black cotton pants, an outfit I had no idea I'd be wearing for the next three days. I grabbed my keys, some cash, and my cell phone, and went out the door and down the stairs. As I stepped outside, I felt an unpleasant shiver of risk, like I was embarking on a creepy, sad adventure, but at no point did I think I should turn back. Once I started out, there was not a chance that I'd turn around. I was propelled by my will—the part of my will that is controlled by my disease.

Outside, I made two rights, went around the block, and came upon a guy hanging out on a stoop. I could see that he was on heroin, the way drug addicts can recognize one another. Now, a person who was in the habit of using would have been paranoid enough—or at least careful enough—to glance over her shoulder to see who might be watching, e.g., the cops. But I'd been totally clean for a year, and it had been six years since I'd been actively using heroin. So, without looking around, I asked the guy if he could help hook me up. He asked me if I was a cop. Slipping right back into a routine from my old using days, I pulled up my sleeve to show him my faded, scarred track marks. (Not proud of those.) He walked to the corner and I followed him. I gave him the money and he took off. I waited for him on Clinton Street and East Broadway. Moments later, he came back holding two small yellow bags.

The minute I took a bag from his hands, several plainclothes police officers appeared out of nowhere and I was surrounded. Before my eyes, an image of my life, the life I'd worked so hard to put back together, sank silently into a pile of gray ash. *Oh shit, it's finally happened.*

Why was I so fucking shocked? It's not like I was going to buy some flowers at the corner bodega. This is what happens to drug addicts when they go out and cop drugs. I knew the risk I was taking, and I took it anyway. I'd gotten away with it before, so I thought I was invincible, but now I was getting caught. I was a dumb-ass, not a victim.

"Put your hands up. Show me what's in your hand. Show me what's in your pocket. Put your hands behind your back." Orders from the police.

I reluctantly unclenched my fist and showed them the drugs. My mind was racing. I reacted like anyone who has ever been pulled over for a speeding ticket or caught shoplifting. I scrambled for whatever words I thought might miraculously change the circumstances. "This is a mistake. You don't understand. This is a fluke. I'm researching a part. I'm not meant to be here. Please." (Note to drug-copping, high-profile actors: when buying crack in New York City, don't tell cops that you're "researching a part." They won't buy it. They will tell the press on you. And the press will relentlessly mock you for it.)

Soon I was in a police van, shackled to another person, glad for only one thing—I hadn't actually used. I was utterly, miserably sober. The cops drove me around for a few hours, picking up more people, before we were all brought to the police station.

Then came the moment that would stay with me forever. As my phone was taken from me, I saw that it was ringing and it was Emily and I couldn't answer it. I knew I would soon have to tell her and my boys about this new low point in my life. Gone was my hard-won custody arrangement. Gone was all that hard work. Gone was my children's trust. My life was officially over. Everything was gone. Gone, gone, gone.

That persistent ring was a broken promise, announcing itself again and again. Then the ringing stopped, and that was even worse.

. . . .

HOW DO YOU pick yourself up, day after day, when people don't believe in you and you have every reason to give up on yourself? How do you survive when you've nearly lost your children for good, when your addictions have led to an arrest, when work becomes hard to find and the life you once expected to lead seems more and more remote?

Only now, years after *A Paper Life,* am I starting to find the answers. After the arrest—and the near relapse that led to it—after all the pain that has come to the surface, my exit wounds are starting to close. Scars have formed and healed. The burden of all that chaos and tragedy has lifted, and I am seeing reasons for everything I've endured. Telling my story has brought me some relief. I feel a lightness I've never known before. And the moment of realization has finally come. I am okay. I am really okay. And no matter what happens, I am going to stay okay. Yeah, I'm whole—well, almost. I'll get to that later.

THIS BOOK IS about rebuilding a life. It's about how I kept going, with a public childhood and a famous father, a public marriage and an acrimonious divorce, a public addiction for fifteen years and an imperfect record of sobriety. It's about how I kept going in the face of criticism, judgment, and my own incomprehensible demoralization. It's about how, after all I went through as a child and an adult, all the trauma and the self-destruction, a decent life emerged. It's about how I realized that there's never a time to give up, not if you have kids and the slightest sense of purpose on the planet. Giving up is not an option. No matter how much others and you yourself condemn you. No matter how close you come to losing who you are.

. . . .

IN *A PAPER LIFE,* I told my story, and it was mine alone—the truth-is-stranger-than-fiction saga of being a child star in a dysfunctional show-biz family. But the story of my recent years is much more universal. This is the story of how I got sober, conquered my addictions once and for all, and am working to preserve that victory one day at a time. It is about the challenges and joys of being a mother; an ex-wife; and a single, middle-age actress. (Yes, I said it.) It's about a woman who was once scared to get close to people but has learned how to be a friend and to trust in intimacy with others.

Rebuilding a life means taking stock of what you have and what you've lost. As hope grew and I reemerged, I saw that there was an important person missing from my life: my father. Daddy. Ours was the most important relationship of my life, and it was nonexistent for nearly twenty years.

More than anything, this is the story of a father and a daughter. When I wrote *A Paper Life,* I realized that there was no fairy-tale ending, that no life, particularly one in which a child is traumatized, is ever perfectly resolved. In the ongoing process of rebuilding my life, it was time to deal with my biggest unresolved issue. My dad. Ryan O'Neal. That strong, compelling movie star who was, at one time, my hero and my savior. Yet we had barely spoken in eight years. Even at my mother's funeral in 1997, we acknowledged each other but did not speak. Now I felt confident, strong, and certain of what I wanted. I was ready to try again, to rebuild my relationship with my father after so much private and public estrangement. And so I began a slow, careful attempt to reconcile with him. That reconciliation ran an uneven path, growing, faltering, and, ultimately, persevering.

When Ryan and I first had the idea to share our efforts to mend our fragmented relationship with a television audience, we both thought long and hard about whether to do it. The risks and pitfalls were obvious—we might reinjure our new, delicate relationship and/or expose our private lives. But the honesty that the camera brings appealed to me. I wanted us to face each other in a harsh spotlight, where we couldn't hide anything, where each of us would have to take responsibility for how we had behaved in the past and who we were in the present. I wanted to force our secrets out into the open. Much as our lives have played out in public and on the screen, I felt the camera, with its unflinching mirror of truth, was the mediator most likely to propel us forward in our journey. My father would have a chance to show that he was not the man who, in a *Vanity Fair* article, said negative things about me and his sons; that he's more than the mug shot seen around the world after he was arrested in 2007 for firing a gun at my brother Griffin. And I would have a chance to show that I'm more than the daughter of someone famous, the wife of someone famous, a drug addict whose children had made it in spite of me, not because of me.

So this tale includes the ups and downs as we tried to forge a new relationship—at times a fraught, emotional, and seemingly doomed effort, but also a funny, surreal glimpse of a father and daughter who made an iconic film together in the early seventies, who've had their problems and still have them, who are celebrities but still regular people, trying to survive as father and daughter as best we can.

. . . .

WHAT DOES IT mean to forgive—literally, physically, emotionally, and spiritually? As far as I'm concerned, my father started me on a rocky path in life. What does it mean to watch a man who hurt you grow older, to see that the years you have left together are diminishing, day by day, and to realize you have to choose between accepting the person he is or letting him go forever? For so many years, I cut my father off, but I finally felt it was time to face him again and try to heal the wounds.

I began this journey thinking that I needed to find a way to let go of the past—that forgetting was the only way to forgive. Parents and kids can make terrible mistakes. But as Ryan and I circled and spun, pulling each other closer and pushing each other away, I found that the past was always with me—always reasserting itself. Sometimes it was melancholy, sometimes hopeful. Sometimes it gave me strength. Sometimes it kept me true. But it always bound me to my father, with a complicated, ordinary, undying love.

Ryan cannot change the past, but in making a TV show about our reconnection, I believed he had the opportunity to give us the present and a future, and that would be the best gift a father could give his daughter.

I was terrified to bring my father back into my life. Ryan can be the most charming, sweet, gentle person in the entire world. I have always wanted to please him. I have always longed to bask in the glow of his acceptance and love. But I remembered his anger, and I still feared it. Still, I decided that if, regardless of my fear, Ryan and I could forgive each other and repair such a damaged relationship, then anyone can, and it would be an effort worth sharing.

And so I am telling everything. The truth. The struggle. The hope. The love. I believe it is the right thing to do, and that it will bring the right outcome, whatever that may be. We are all dealt different hands, and some are tougher than others to survive. There are traumas and there is damage that create seemingly insurmountable hurdles. But I am as determined to move forward as I've ever been. *You can and must survive, no matter what.* That's my motto. There is always hope.

PART I

FRACTURES

CHAPTER ONE
OUTSIDE AND IN

I SPENT THE night of the arrest in a jail on the Lower East Side. I talked on the pay phone as long as I could, with my lawyer and with my boyfriend, Ron, who promised to talk to Emily. Then I lay on a bare foam pad, spooning with a pregnant prostitute, pretending to sleep while reliving the nightmare I had brought on myself. *How had this happened? How had I gone wrong again?*

The next morning I was released from jail, and there were a thousand press people waiting for me. I soon found out that the cover of that day's *New York Post* announced that I'd been arrested. Great. My oldest child, Kevin, had finished college and was working at a restaurant while he applied to grad schools. My middle child, Sean, was in Paris on a summer trip. Emily was in high school in New York. All I could think about was what this news would do to them. How horribly embarrassing for everybody. Why did I have to keep embarrassing them?

I hurried into my lawyer Jodi's Prius, and she told me I couldn't return to my apartment—the press was there, too. I tried to contact my best friend, Kyle, on the phone, but it was Monday. Kyle, a colorist at a top hair salon, was unreachable. So I asked Jodi to drive me across town to my friends Hunter and Perry's apartment.

Hunter and Perry were among my closest friends while I was in New York, but because of my inability to bond with people, I kept even them at arm's length, like everyone else. When I got to their house, I went into a bedroom and closed the door. Alone, I tried to process what was happening in my life. Alone—the only way I knew to endure the grief and anguish I was suffering. Again, I asked myself: *How had this happened?*

The answer wasn't black-and-white—it never is. I had been dedicated to sobriety for more than a decade, since 1994. I went to Alcoholics Anonymous meetings. I had a sponsor to guide me through the twelve steps: Sandy. Sandy is a gentle, loving person. She has long hair parted down the middle, which, combined with her softness, makes her look like the Virgin Mary. She had helped me with my sense of self, and was teaching me to forgive myself. After the conflicted relationships I had had with my mother and other women through the years, Sandy was a very positive force in my life. I had a true friend in Kyle, who knew me better than anyone. I was complying with my divorce judge's orders to drug-test biweekly, with a monitor in the room with me to prove I wasn't cheating. I had a reliable and fulfilling routine, including being with my children on the weekends. With Emily, because she was the youngest, I had immediately seen the positive impact of our time together.

Life wasn't perfect, but by June 2008, I felt I was really becoming the woman I had always wanted to be.

But the scary truth about addiction is that it doesn't need a precipitating event. There is a switch in my head that, for seemingly arbitrary and insignificant reasons, can flip, and when it does, all the joy I've found in being sober slips out of reach. The switch flips and the voice starts playing: *Why don't I just use today? Why not?*

The longer I maintained my sobriety, the healthier I would be. Time, I would discover, was one of the great rewards of staying sober. Experiencing the richness of life without substances was a reward in itself. The obsession to use faded. Nothing can compare to how great things are when I am sober. It was so great to be accountable, to achieve my goals, to have my kids trust me and not worry if I didn't answer my phone every time they called. But at the time of the arrest, my sobriety was still relatively young and immature. I wasn't aware of how easily I could slip. I hadn't developed the instinct to call my sponsor before making the dumb choice to get loaded. I hadn't instituted enough safeguards—friends, meetings, obligations—to protect me from my weakest self.

Where did that weakness come from? Someone once told me that I am always just a little bit sad. There is truth to that. From the time I was little, I have carried a sadness for how things ended with my family—with both my mother and my father, though in different ways.

That recurring sadness wasn't the only trigger. I had been suffering from debilitating nerve damage in my neck caused by a terrible car accident in 1976, after which my body was never the same. I had a chronic degenerative disk disease. I'd undergone one surgery and would end up having two more. The pain radiated from my neck to the tips of my fingers. It seemed unfair, because who deserves to be in that kind of pain? Despite the risks, which I knew as well as anybody else, I was prescribed pain meds by the doctor. I'd periodically taken them without abusing them. But this time, for some reason, taking a pill for my neck pain flipped a switch. That's the cunning and baffling thing about addiction: it gets you when you least expect it.

That said, it was not surprising that the arrest happened on a Sunday. Sundays were always my saddest, loneliest days. At the end of the weekends, my three kids had always gone back to John. Now it was just Emily, the last one still in high school, who returned to her father on Sunday nights. That fateful Sunday, one moment, I was sitting on my couch, missing all three of my kids. The next minute, I was out the door, trying to score some drugs. If it was crack I found, then it was crack I would use. *Sure, this time, why not throw my life away? It's Sunday. I have no kids, no friends, no life!* I did, of course, have all of these things.

BEING IN JAIL was the most horrible moment I'd had as a woman and a mother. The whole world now knew that I had drug problems. I was embarrassed for my children. What were the parents of their friends saying to them? How was my ex-husband going to handle it with them? I can't stress enough how horrible I felt realizing what this would do to my teenage daughter and to my sons, who were young adults. What I was doing was illegal. And I was not just breaking laws, being irresponsible, damaging myself. The arrest shone a light on my real problem—the biggest and most powerful problem of all, always and only—the consequences of my addiction in the lives of my children. My children. I'm a mother. This was not what I wanted for them.

All this is what I should have been thinking when I was walking down that street, on the verge of breaking my sobriety. Obviously.

I know this sounds strange, but being arrested was scarier for me than when I used to cop heroin on the street. As a child I fell out of trees; I was thrown from a car; I broke my arm and my foot; I had been paddled, switched, and sexually abused. After all that, the idea of taking a drug was just not that big a deal. In fact, it made perfect sense. What better way to bear the mess of my life? But the arrest, more than anything I'd ever experienced, forced me to feel the effect on my beautiful children.

This had been a problem all along, of course, but everyone has a line they won't cross, and the arrest was the wake-up call I needed: using drugs was no longer an option for me. It had devastating, long-term effects on my children—their sense of self, of safety, of who their mother is, of how comfortable they are with me. For all the misery and self-flagellation of being arrested, something good happened in that jail cell. Something that changed me forever. I was scared straight.

THE FIRST THING I did when I got to Hunter and Perry's house was call Emily to apologize and see if she was all right. She just said, "I'm so glad you're okay. I'm glad you didn't use." The boys felt the same way. They were perfect, so loving, generous, accepting, forgiving. They didn't take the arrest nearly as hard as I did. They had been through enough to understand the disease of addiction. They got it. All that mattered to them was that I didn't fall back into the cycle of using. Because they had spent so many years worrying that I would die, the arrest itself wasn't that big a deal for them. It took a few weeks for my ex-husband to feel comfortable enough for me to see Emily, but he didn't go to court to try to suspend her visitations. He made it clear to me that this was a considered decision; he meant it as a gesture of faith, and I appreciated it. When Kyle and I finally spoke, he was very upset and sad. The press had been calling him to ask about me. Did I go to the salon loaded? He had told them of course not. Now he asked if I would come stay with him, or if there was anything else he could do.

That was the common thread. All around me, I found love and saw glimmers of hope. I was given love, support, and forgiveness. The work I had done to clean up my life was still in place. The scaffold of sobriety was still standing. It was the easiest thing in the world to keep on building.

I ultimately came to see the arrest as a blessing in disguise. Sometimes God does for us what we cannot do for ourselves. I was not meant to use those drugs that day. Instead, I lived through twenty-four hours of hell in jail, and I know I'll never be there again. I saw how my addiction had wrecked everything in my life, but now, taking it one day at a time, I would never use again. I was done. And with that realization, I looked ahead and saw the beautiful, wonderful opportunity of a new life.

I JUMPED BACK in with both feet, ready to go to any length for my sobriety. Within two days of my arrest, I was speaking at a meeting for cocaine addicts. Without missing any work, I returned to the set of the show *Rescue Me*, a series starring Denis Leary about the lives of a group of New York City firefighters, in which I played the part of Denis's sister, Maggie Gavin, in the ensemble cast.

There were a lot of actors on the set, a lot of Irish boys, and I seemed to fit in pretty well. We felt like a family. I had been with the show for four years at that point—what had started as a two-day part had grown into a series regular. Nonetheless, when I came back to the set after having been arrested, I was nervous. There was tension—I could feel everyone wondering if I was okay. Denis, who wasn't in that day's scene with me, appeared on set my first day back. I knew he was only there to support me and see if everything was okay. He had already gone on *The View* to say that I'd never been late, I'd never missed a day of work, and that he would work with me again in two seconds. He had called me and asked, "Tates, you okay? You all right there, Tates?" I was determined to show him and the others that they were right to trust and believe in me.

The scene I had to do was not an easy one. I was supposed to try to seduce a guy in a wheelchair at the VA hospital in Staten Island. My character, Maggie, was a loose drunk. People may have joked, "Art imitates life, huh?" Not so much because I go around seducing the disabled—more the drunk part. But even at my worst, I was never a rough, drunk broad. And now I felt more sensitive and careful than ever. I did my scene and went home.

Two weeks later, I had my second neck surgery.

A FEW MONTHS after I recovered from the surgery, it was time to see Emily off to her first year of college. John and I took her to her school in Northern California together, as a family. My ex-husband and I had been at war for a long time. That trip was a big deal for us. The three of us had the typical awkward meeting with her roommates' families, and then we trouped to Bed Bath & Beyond to buy miscellany for Emily's dorm room. I knew having both of her parents there together, managing to keep the peace, meant a lot to Emily. After we said our good-byes to our youngest child, John and I flew from San Francisco to L.A., sitting on the plane side by side. We hadn't sat that close for more than a decade. It was awkward, to be sure, but there was finally some peace after years of acrimony.

That trip marked the end of an era. I had stayed in New York for more than a decade after my divorce to see my children through elementary and high school, and they were thriving. Kevin had finished Skidmore and been accepted to Columbia for grad school. Sean was at Occidental. And now Emily was settling into the next phase of her life. I was very proud of them. And I saw what I had to do for myself. The time had come to make a change. I was ready to come home. To be found.

CHAPTER TWO

HOME AGAIN

I HAD LONG been homesick for California. Living on the Lower East
Side, I was unsettled by the jackhammering and the hustle-bustle
of sidewalks crowded with people from all walks of life. Cigarette
smoke flowed from the street through my first-floor window, a daily
assault. But my alienation from New York ran deeper than the everyday discomforts.

My first eight years in New York were spent married, being a
young mother, traveling internationally with John. New York had
done some good work on me. It taught me how to be forthright, to
look people straight in the eye, to be a strong woman of substance
and intellect. But during my marriage and the fifteen years that followed, I'd really never found a core group of friends.

Sure, there was Kyle. He'd been processing my hair at the Oscar

Blandi Salon for two years before we finally decided to go to a screening together. I think one of the first screenings we went to was *Frozen River* with Melissa Leo. For some reason, the theater was freezing cold, which made the setting feel a little too real, but we liked the movie.

Kyle is a beautiful young gay man from Long Island, though you'd never know the Long Island bit because he took voice lessons to lose his heavy accent. He is one of six children from an Irish-Italian family. We may not have had much in common on the surface, but the more time we spent with each other the closer we became. I knew instinctively that I could trust him. Kyle would never judge or condemn me for my addictions. He would never turn his back on me. Part of the healing process for me was feeling unconditionally loved, and Kyle and I found that kind of love in each other. And, less critical for the friendship, he is a true genius with hair color.

Kyle was a blessing. Beyond him, I had my social group of friends, and, yes, I had friends from AA, but true intimacy was always a challenge for me. There were few people I would call in a pinch, even when, like Kyle and Hunter and Perry, I knew they would be there for me. (And by *in a pinch* I mean *plagued by the soul-draining darkness that has been with me since I was born*. Isn't that what everyone means by *in a pinch*?) Isolation is something I bring on myself without realizing it. I grew up without a family structure or a proper support system. I had no formal schooling and no peer group. There is a difference between loneliness and being alone, but I'm so used to both that I can't always tell them apart. When I'm lonely, I don't exactly notice and do something about it. Even when people reach out to me, I can be apprehensive. In New York, there were always people who would have been my friends, true friends, but, particularly as the series *Rescue Me* came to a close, I felt the pull of L.A., where I had stronger connections than anyplace else. Or so I thought.

My oldest son, Kevin, was still in New York, which made it an especially hard decision. It would be tough to leave him. But my other two children were on the West Coast now. They were all too old for me to keep them in the tight cluster I wanted. And so it was time to go home to the sea and the mountains and to explore the memories. Good or bad, they were my memories.

I planned to leave New York within weeks of taking Emily to college, so before we both left, she and I had a farewell dinner with Kevin and his girlfriend, Caroline, at a restaurant on the Lower East Side.

I looked at my two children across the table, my oldest and my youngest. Kevin is tall—six foot four—with blond hair and green eyes, and my coloring. He lives with his girlfriend, Caroline, and their terrier, Nate. Kevin is deeply dedicated to his independence and making a life outside the shadow of his famous parents. It's exciting and fun to watch him.

Emily has snow-white skin with freckles, long, dark, curly hair, a round Irish face, and the sweetest spirit a mother could wish for. She is always well-dressed in her own unique style she likes to call grunge-glam. Emily is a caregiver, the kind of girl people go to with their problems, but as her mother, I can't help reminding her to take care of her own needs first.

Kevin and I had never lived so far away from each other. For college, he went to Skidmore in upstate New York, where it was easy for me to visit him all the time. We were all used to me traveling a lot, and it didn't occur to us that this move might feel any different. Much as I hoped L.A. would work out for me, Emily and I both kept saying, "We'll be back!" I figured that as soon as I'd earned the money I needed to put myself back on stable financial footing, I'd come back to visit or fly Kevin out to see me. I still had my New York apartment and no plans to sell it. As for Kevin, if he had any reservations about my departure, he didn't say so. In the McEnroe family, they sometimes say, "The boys aren't so good with their words." Kevin is one of those boys. But my guess is that the reality of my departure didn't hit him that night. It hadn't really hit me, either. None of us felt that the move was going to be permanent.

IN SPITE OF all the allegations and alienation, in some way, going home meant returning to Ryan. It took me a few months to find an apartment and pack all my things. All the while, my father was on my mind. My role on *Rescue Me* was finished except for the finale, for which I would fly back to New York. I moved in the summer of 2009 and set about reestablishing a life in the city where my father had been the center of my world.

One of my first orders of business in L.A. was attending an AA meeting. I went to a morning meeting in Beverly Hills that I had gone to on many previous visits to L.A. As I took my seat and watched people filter in, I noticed an attractive woman who seemed to know everyone at the meeting. After the meeting, I saw the same woman talking with a circle of women. She seemed very involved and invested in their lives. I could tell that she was their sponsor, and I imagined she was a good one if she was actively helping this many women stay sober. I was curious. I went up to her and introduced myself. Her name was Patty. She was dark-skinned, with long hair and a va-va-voom body, but tasteful style. It was a summer night, and she was wearing a pretty cotton dress with red flowers on it, which looked like a vintage dress from the forties. I told her I really liked the dress. She told me a bit about herself, and then I said, "I'm looking for a sponsor." After a brief conversation, we exchanged phone numbers.

The next morning I called Patty, and a few days after that we met at her place in Beverly Hills to talk. Patty's apartment was comfortable and laid-back, with a comfy couch, cats that meowed a lot, and a Chihuahua named Pepito.

Patty asked me what I was hoping for in a sponsor. I said I was looking for someone who could walk me through the steps. I wanted to find a woman who would be interested in my recovery and life, but who wouldn't be distracted by who I've been, or seem like I am, or the life that I appeared to have lived.

Patty was around my age, which I liked. She hadn't had children, but I could instantly see that she would focus on our similarities, not our differences. I recognized a very good, strong spirit in Patty. I didn't get the sense that she'd judge me, or compare us, or feel threatened by me. She was open and caring, maternal and protective. She was kind but also careful.

We agreed to give it a go, and from then on Patty and I talked on the phone every day. Sometimes sponsors expect their sponsees to call them. It becomes something of a power play for them to have a protégé whose responsibility it is to report to them. That dynamic doesn't work for me, especially since my inclination is not to reach out for help, even when I should. Patty doesn't play that game. We call each other, and it doesn't matter to either of us who dials the phone. We're not there for a power play. I'm there for an alcohol and drug problem. Finding Patty was my first step toward building a stable, sober life in L.A.

One of the other early phone calls I made when I was getting my footing in L.A. was to my old friend Tony. Tony and I had known each other since we were ten and went to the same school. In our teens, we'd go to the famous old-school Beverly Hills deli Nate and Al's, and drive around doing all the silly things that fifteen-year-olds do, blowing off school and going to the beach together.

Growing up, we all knew that Tony was gay, but he wasn't ready to tell his parents. He finally came out of the closet in his mid-thirties. We'd stayed in touch over all the years. Tony has a big personality. He's funny and has a lot of energy, so he brings a certain amount of excitement with him to even the most mundane lunch date. I've always been drawn to people like that, and I do best, it seems, with gay men.

Once Tony and I reconnected, we took up where we'd left off. He was also sober, although he was having trouble staying so, and we started going to a meeting together every day. We had lunch and dinner all the time. I thought, *Okay, great. At least I have one person here whom I know and can talk to, who is sober. Or at least trying his best.*

Over the next six months, I settled into my new life, attending meetings every day, going to the gym, taking my dog for walks, spending time with my son Sean, reconnecting with old friends and trying to meet new ones, and auditioning.

CHAPTER THREE

FATHER AND SON

A SERIES OF events led me back to Ryan, but most of all, it was my younger son, Sean. Ryan and I had been estranged for years and years. It began in 1979, when I was fifteen years old and he moved out of the house; continued through the rest of my teens; and kept on during my marriage to John, who didn't trust Ryan as far as he could throw him. Given John's strong personality, it was easier for me just to have little contact with Ryan for most of our eight-year marriage, which lasted from 1986 to 1994. Most recently, the scandal that came between us was my publication of *A Paper Life*, which exposed to the world for the first time how Ryan had treated me when I was growing up. Writing the book was torture, but being on the other end of it can't have been pleasant. Needless to say, my father didn't call to apologize and make amends. We didn't speak directly about the content of *A Paper Life*—my father claimed not to have read it—but I knew full well what his reaction was to the book's revelations. He was angry. How dare I talk about our personal lives that way? I had always been warned against that—warnings so powerful that they wove themselves permanently into my young brain. He was and is a private man. Even now, with my father's tentative consent to write this book, I worry about hurting and upsetting him.

I didn't intend *A Paper Life* to be an attack on Ryan, but I wasn't surprised that he sought to defend himself. Everything that I described in the book Ryan denied to the press, and we never spoke of it. Since the publication of *A Paper Life* until very recently, I harbored anger for all that had happened, and my best guess was that he was equally angry at my having exposed it.

Those are the broad brushstrokes of Ryan's and my estrangement, but my relationship with my father is a canvas layered with years of paint in myriad colors—some harsh and sharp lines, some gentle and curved, some light, some dark. As new strokes are added, the overall tone of the painting shifts. No single stroke tells the whole story, but maybe some of the smallest, most muted corners of the picture can best hint at the whole.

In 1994, I entered Hazelden for my first trip to rehab. I'd been addicted to heroin for several months. It was a very rough time. I wanted to be off heroin. But heroin was also the only thing that made me feel like I was meant to be alive. Ever since my divorce earlier that year, my life had tumbled quickly and steeply downhill. Heroin was the only way I had found to feel inner peace. It was the sole antidote to my pain, and yet it was ruining everything: my career, my relationship with my kids, my life. I couldn't wrap my head around that fucking contradiction. Anyone who had been through what I'd endured, and found a way to take away the pain, would have to understand that I couldn't let go of it. I had tried suicide three times without success. Without killing myself, taking the drug was the only way to endure. It was the best I could do.

I spent Christmas at Hazelden with snow up to the sky, shivering my ass off, not knowing how I'd ended up there. I was alone and needed my family. What family? I called Ryan. I don't know exactly what kind of support I was hoping to get from him. But all he said was, "Don't blame me for the fact that you're smoking the dragon." The phone went dead. My dad never did make a habit of saying good-bye. I stared at the disconnected phone, listening to the dull dial tone, having a conversation in my head. *Hang in there, Tatey, your dad loves you.*

Love you too, Dad, I said to the empty phone. *And P.S., while we're on the subject, the proper terminology is "chasing the dragon."* He was right. This mess was my fault. But it was hard to hear him say it that way. For me, the alienation came from moments like that, seemingly inconsequential brushstrokes that further shadowed already dim corners of my being.

As for my father, he saw things in more black-and-white terms. He was angry and hurt that I'd chosen to distance myself from him in the first place. He did not participate in my rehab process and, eventually, I emerged. The 2004 publication of *A Paper Life* was just another black mark against me, as far as he was concerned. But it was a necessary phase in the healing process for me. I *needed* the truth to be told. Since then, my father and I had had only small encounters, fraught events where we never addressed what had come between us, and it seemed like that was how we would go on in perpetuity. He later would say that he erased me.

Until: "May I have Grandpa's phone number?" It was Sean. My twenty-year-old son, Sean, had met Ryan only a couple of times in his young life. A decade earlier, around the time my mother passed away in 1997, we had taken a family trip to Hawaii together when the kids were really little—me, the three kids, Ryan, Farrah, and their son (my half-brother), Redmond—and around the same time, we'd spent a few weekends out at Ryan's beach house in Malibu. But for the most part, Ryan was a stranger to Sean and his siblings, a larger-than-life figure he knew from Ryan's movies, from magazines, and from family photos. Now Sean was studying theater at Occidental College, in L.A. He was a third-generation actor and had been yearning for a connection to his roots, to the family vocation, to the O'Neal family in general. He wanted to experience the connection with my side of the family.

I thought long and hard about the decision to make the introduction. I asked God to guide me toward the right answer. Part of me had always thought the kids needed to have relationships with my family. But, as my ex-husband had put it more than once, "No, actually, they don't." Fair enough. My family was fractured, a stew of drama, drugs, violence, and tragedy. Only four years earlier my father and my brother Griffin had been in the news for an epic fight that ended in gunshots and my dad's arrest. Nobody knew my father's faults better than I. But he was older now. I hoped, the way a daughter does, with hope against hope, that Ryan had changed. Maybe he would surprise me. Maybe when his young grandson called—this handsome, worthy young man who was so ready to love his grandfather—Ryan would rise to the occasion.

My heart wanted Sean to find a strong male role model in Ryan. And I missed my father. Our good years together in Los Angeles—

when he took custody of me and Griffin, and Ryan and I made *Paper Moon*—had been some of my happiest. Even when we weren't speaking, I always felt his presence. He was the most important man in my life, forever.

I did it. For better or worse, I gave Sean his grandfather Ryan's phone number, a number I myself hadn't called in years.

NOT LONG AFTER I gave him Ryan's phone number, Sean reported that he and Ryan had gone out to dinner, and that it had gone well. As I rebuilt my life in L.A., Sean and Ryan started spending more time together, reading lines, walking on the beach, playing Frisbee, taking saunas at Ryan's house in Malibu. Even though nothing was explicit, it was as if Ryan and I were communicating again, through Sean.

I was glad to hear how well things were going between the two of them, but I tracked Sean's experience carefully. He didn't really know who he was dealing with when it came to my father. That charm might give way to anger at any moment. It was impossible for anyone who hadn't experienced it firsthand to superimpose the behavior I could describe on a man who could be so soft, so caring, so sensitive, so charming. Nothing was as real as when it happened, that tsunami of utter transformation. I wanted to protect Sean, so I told him what I thought he needed to know, but I also wanted to give Ryan the benefit of the doubt. I imagined in my mind that Ryan had mellowed, that the sharp edges I remembered had eroded.

Sean seemed happy, and that was what mattered. He was old enough to know what was good for him, and this was a connection that he needed in his life. Amazingly, after all these years, he appeared to be building a healthy relationship with his grandfather. I was back in L.A. Sean and Ryan were spending time together. Ryan and I were circling closer and closer.

And then, on June 25, 2009, Farrah died.

CHAPTER FOUR
IS THAT YOU?

THE MEMORIES I have of Farrah are fragments—the sharp, scattered pieces of a broken childhood. Harmless, even childlike though she was, I could not help but secretly resent her presence in our lives. I hadn't had anyone acting as a mother figure or female role model for years, and the job requirements were minimal. Throughout most of my young life, nobody had bothered to care what—or even if—I ate. But in 1979, when Farrah entered our lives, Griffin and I were involuntarily emancipated. When I phoned my father to complain about his absence from the beach house, Ryan said, "What? You're fifteen. What's the problem?"

Farrah and my father assumed I was an adult (I'd acted like one since I was nine), and that Griffin, who was a year younger than me, and I had no need for supervision. There was probably a housekeeper who stocked the refrigerator, but she must have kept out of our way, because I don't remember her. We smoked pot. Griffin surfed while I swam. One time, the two of us drove ourselves to Big Sur, contemplating a more permanent move. But that idea didn't last. Mostly, there was a lot of watching TV, feeling lonely, wondering what purpose we had on earth.

When we did see Ryan and Farrah, it seemed clear to my young eyes that my father would prefer that Farrah and I stay apart. He admits it—joking that he was afraid we would conspire against him. Even in later years, his focus never stopped being on Farrah, and he found the idea that I was sensitive about that weird, even sacrilegious. How dare I? Ryan tells me that they once took me to the dermatologist for a mole or something when I was sixteen, his "proof" that they fulfilled parental duties, but I don't remember that.

There was not a cruel bone in Farrah's body. She just had no notion of what she could or should do about these rogue children who were, to all appearances, an incidental, remote component of her relationship with Ryan. Soon after my phone call asking my dad to come home, he and my brother had an infamous fight in which my brother lost a tooth.

Much as I had looked at Farrah with admiration and wonder, she had also suddenly and permanently come between me and my father. Innocent bystander though she may have been, I could never separate Farrah from that experience.

IN 2006, WHEN my brother Griffin first told me that Farrah had been diagnosed with cancer, I felt somewhat distanced from the news. I knew it was terribly sad for my father, but I was still figuring out what Farrah meant to me: a mother, an icon, my father's girlfriend. No matter what, I still felt terrible grief that she was so ill. I had really loved her.

A year after Farrah's diagnosis, during a break from *Rescue Me,* I was in San Diego working on a miniseries. Griffin, who was always the bad-news-bearer of the family (not to be confused with the Bad News Bear of the family), called to let me know that Farrah's cancer was getting worse. It was serious. If I wanted to say good-bye, I had better go see her soon. It would be as much of a hello as a good-bye.

I called Farrah to see how she was and to ask if I could visit. She said, "Sure, come see me." I thought that was sweet, so I drove my rented Kia to her grand apartment building on Wilshire Boulevard, bringing food and flowers and all of my good thoughts.

When I entered Farrah's bedroom, what struck me first was how gorgeous she still was. I hadn't seen her for many years, and, sick as she was, she looked more glamorous than ever. She lived and died a true beauty. I sat down on her bed and talked with her, saying nothing about our complicated history, just general, quiet talk about her illness and how she was fighting it. I held her hands and gave her love. We shared a mutual respect, and it was monumental that we were seeing each other, alone, something that had never really happened before. Being at Farrah's bedside meant that I wasn't afraid of my father anymore. I needed to show her I was no longer the scared and envious girl she'd first met; I wanted to show her the woman I'd become. And so we sat together, accepting the bond that could have been but never was. It was my last and only moment with Farrah before she died, peaceful and sad.

In June 2009, two years after that visit, I found out that Farrah had died, from her best friend, Alana Stewart. Griffin, my news-bearer, had been ostracized after he and our dad had had that epic gun fight. Alana let me know that there was going to be a private funeral. I was on my way to L.A. anyway—the lease on my new apartment started the day before the funeral. But more to the point, I thought that the occasion would offer some kind of an opening for me to reconnect with my dad. It would be the first time in years that I'd see him without Farrah. I wanted to be there for him, and I thought we might find our long-lost connection. It was worth a shot.

I called my father and left a message to ask if I could attend the funeral. Through Alana and Sean, I got Ryan's okay to come.

I WALKED INTO Farrah's funeral awash in a mix of emotions: deeply sad for the loss, nervous to see my father. I knew that Redmond had been released from jail to attend, but that he would be in shackles. There would be a lot of people attending who were strangers to me, people from the last twenty-five years of my father and Farrah's life. I had to be brave. I brought Ron Castellano, my ex-boyfriend. He and I were still dear friends, having dated intermittently over the past three and a half years. He had come with me from New York to help me get settled in my new place, and I felt very safe around him.

As I walked into the church, I heard someone say that Griffin was outside, trying to come in. It pained me to hear that. What I didn't know at the time was that my dad had forbidden Griffin from attending the funeral. It was just like Griffin to show up regardless. He has never cared about how he's perceived. I don't judge him, or any of my brothers, for whatever ways they've found to survive. In some way maybe I was the luckiest, because I had *A Paper Moon* and an Oscar to buoy me along; Patrick, Griffin, and Redmond didn't have those tangibles.

Gathered in the pews, I saw many faces I hadn't seen in a long time. My uncle Kevin and his wife were there, with their son Garrett. I saw my half-brother Patrick. Dillan, Griffin's seventeen-year-old daughter, had come in alone, while Griffin, his wife, Jojo, and their baby waited outside. There was Zetta, my former accountant who had worked for our family since the seventies; Ron Meyer, my old friend from Hollywood; Mela, a family friend who was Farrah's hairdresser. Marianne Williamson, the famous life coach, was one of the speakers at the service. It was quite the emotional onslaught.

During the ceremony I sat there, crying quietly. I thought about all that might have been. What I'd never been able to achieve with Farrah as a stepdaughter or even as a friend. All we had was that one short but poignant meeting on her deathbed. And, apparently, a long-ago trip to the dermatologist.

Immediately after the ceremony people lined up outside to give their condolences to Ryan. I saw him up ahead. There he was, my father. He had his sunglasses on, but I could see that he was crying. He seemed distraught. Tears sprang to my eyes. Much had happened to me in recent years—a marriage, three children, a painful divorce, years of struggling with addiction and achieving sobriety—all major life milestones. I was finally seeing my estranged father, watching him mourn the death of the woman who had unwittingly come between us so long ago. It was a strange, intense moment.

I joined the line to give my father a hug. I wished we'd stayed a family. I wanted to start anew, to build the relationship I always wanted us to have. I hoped to be a shoulder he could lean on.

There was a breeze in the air that day. My hair was long and blond, and as I reached my father, it kind of got caught flowing across my face. With my face partially hidden, my father grabbed me and pulled me in. It seemed slightly intimate. I had no idea what to expect, but he said, "Hey, baby, got a drink on you? Want to get out of here?" Was it possible that my own father didn't recognize me? It *had* been a pretty long time.

I said, "Dad, Dad. It's Tatum. It's me, Tatum. Your daughter."

My father took a step backward and I saw the light enter his eyes. "Tatum. Oh my God, hi, baby. I didn't recognize you." Through it all, his tears were flowing. What a mess. How surreal.

Nonetheless, we hugged and were able to talk, slightly awkwardly. It was a sad occasion for sure, but a reunion nonetheless. Circumstances aside, I was happy to see him.

When I was a kid, I couldn't have loved a person more than I'd loved my father—Ryan, Daddy, Papa, Dad. He was my everything—my world. When my father and I stopped being close, I felt like I'd lost a limb, like I wasn't a whole person anymore.

Now my dad was heartbroken. The love of his life was gone. Although he looked the same to me, he seemed more vulnerable. Meanwhile, I was healthy, happy, and living in L.A. I was enjoying the sunlight and the mountains and the sea and the space, the meetings, my old friends—and the absence of foot traffic! And jackhammering! To be fair to Manhattan, the L.A. car traffic was a bitch. Nonetheless, my outlook had changed. We had been estranged for roughly twenty years, but it was really thirty if you started counting from when he met Farrah in 1979. I had been through more than my share of hardships, and I was ready to harness them into something positive for my father and me. Would that be possible, given all that had passed between us? I wanted to give it a try.

Evolving in the heart of this moment of reunion was the belief that I was finally strong enough, spiritually and emotionally, to find the beauty and humanity in the man, to keep the light, and to overlook the difficult past in order to have a precious future with him. I wanted my dad to feel like he had a family again. At this stage in his life, he deserved that, despite the problems of the past. He had an enormous heart. And I needed my father. I needed to throw down the gauntlet, to wave a peace flag. I wanted his love even if it came with limitations and risks. As we talked, that first tentative exchange, I started to believe that I possessed the strength of will and spirit to redeem us.

We hugged, somewhat awkwardly, as we said good-bye, but I resolved to see him again. A month after the funeral I was shopping at Whole Foods, picking out organic fruits and veggies. As I poked at the pears, I thought about how we had lost Farrah, and I couldn't help wondering what would happen if Ryan got sick. How would I feel? Would I cope? Would I question myself and my actions? Or lack thereof? When my mother had died in my arms, of advanced lung cancer in 1997, a lot of our issues were left unresolved. If Ryan were to pass away soon, I would be in the same place, wondering what we might have had, what I might have come to understand. Would I feel like I had given it my best effort? I did not want to live with that regret.

I'd been to loads of 12-step meetings and umpteen hours of therapy, enough to follow through on the germinating idea of reconciling with Ryan. What did I want our relationship to look like as we both grew older? To ignore the opportunity was not fair to my kids. I owed them a chance to know their grandfather. Sean, who was still in college, had been spending weekends out at the beach with his grandpa (as he called my father, to Ryan's chagrin). All reports from Sean were good. Grandpa has been great. Grandpa is being really nice to me. We're going to parties. We're going to events. I was glad Sean was seeing the part of my father that I loved. At his best, I knew Ryan to be a compelling presence. Authentic. Deep. Wonderful. Kind. Gentle. There is a charm about him that no one else has.

I ran the idea of reconciling with Ryan past Kevin and Emily. Sean, who knew Ryan now, wanted us to get together with an eye toward patching things up. Unlike Sean, Kevin and Emily were mostly apprehensive, and with reason. They knew that when all three of them had been little, I had taken them to the beach house on an experimental visit to see their grandfather. There had been an incident while I was out on the beach—a fight that the children witnessed between Griffin and Ryan, during which a hammer was thrown. Alarmed, John had sought some kind of legal order that mandated that the kids could not be left with my father unless there was another adult present. After that the children had little contact with their grandfather, but all of my children had witnessed, from the periphery, the publication of *A Paper Life*. Though they hadn't read it—wisely recognizing that it might be too much information—they knew that I'd made a damning representation of what my life was like. Kevin and Emily worried that the outcome I hoped for with Ryan now might be impossible.

Nonetheless, I wanted my children to know their legacy: where I came from, and that they were O'Neals as much as McEnroes. My kids needed to know both sides of their family to be well-rounded people. If they saw me pursue a relationship with Ryan, they would always know that I did it for a reason: love. And if, at any point down the road, they found reason to stop talking to John or me, they would learn from my example that there was always a way to come back, to be brave enough to forgive.

When I got to the parking lot of Whole Foods—an odd location for revelations, but so it goes—I stopped at the door to my car and thought, *It's now or never.* I felt somehow that I'd healed enough. I was no longer bitter about how Ryan had raised—and failed to raise—me. I could forgive him for the choices he'd made. I was now a woman in charge of my own life, and I wasn't going to let the past haunt me anymore. I was ready to make my move. I got in my car and called my father.

CHAPTER FIVE

RECONCILIATION

FOR ALL THE strife between me and my father, there was a powerful bond between us. The happiest years of my life were the first ones that I spent living with him.

As little kids, Griffin and I only saw Ryan when he'd come and take us to the pony rides in West Hollywood. When we were little, there was a fair on the site of what is now a mall—the monolithic Beverly Center. When my parents first separated, my father, having no better ideas, brought us to the pony rides every weekend. I rode Goldie, the same pony that my father had ridden when he was a kid.

My dad tells a story of how one day, on our way to the fair, I was in the passenger seat and Griffin was in the backseat. I was three or four years old, and I was sucking my thumb. I asked my father why he had left us and our mother, where he had gone. To change the subject, he said, "You have to stop sucking your thumb."

I said, "How much will you give me?" Just like Addie, the character I would play four or five years later in *Paper Moon*.

Ryan said, "I'll give you a dollar when you've stopped."

I said, "How about half now, half after I stop?" My father gave me fifty cents, and I never sucked my thumb again.

As my father tells it, he thought being a parent was that easy. Even though there's something sad and sweet about Ryan trying to replicate happy moments from his childhood by introducing me and Griffin to Goldie, he had no clue that it takes more than pony rides and a bribe to raise a kid.

My mother was a warm, loving person and a talented actress—who knows what she might have been if she hadn't suffered the tragic loss of her immediate family at a very young age? There were major reasons for her addictions. But, as it was, she wasn't able to raise us properly. We were struggling, scrawny weeds, with barely enough water to grow. My father was funny and warm, handsome and rich. I set my sights on him. Who wouldn't? When he showed up for his weekend visits, I would start begging him to come back before he'd even left. The rest of the time, I'd wish and wait for him. I prayed for him to come save me, to bring me to live with him in his beach house.

In 1971, when I was seven years old, my dream finally came true. My father rescued me and Griffin, and for several years he provided the water we needed to survive.

Salvation wasn't immediate. When my father first wrested custody from my mother, part of his agreement with her was that he would send us to boarding school. The place they picked was the ironically named Tree Haven in Tucson, Arizona, a school for troubled kids. Dennis Ketcham, the inspiration for the cartoon strip

Dennis the Menace, had been a student. I took up stealing there, a habit I wouldn't drop for a number of years.

Ryan says that once, when he was on location in Houston, he took some time off to visit me at school and found me living with the infants—they'd put me there because there was nothing I could steal from the babies. (Infants at a school for troubled kids? I'll have to ask my dad where he came up with that one.) When his limo pulled away from the school, I chased after the car barefoot, with a bunch of kids, like a pack of starving dogs hoping for a bone.

My father had hated his own boarding school experience, but he assumed it would work out for me and Griffin as it eventually had for him. Still, the image of us chasing the car stayed with him, and when Peter Bogdanovich, who had already directed my father in *What's Up, Doc?,* called Ryan to tell him he had a script with a role for a little girl, he saw a way to get me out of that school.

As Ryan tells it, he arranged for me to fly to L.A. to meet with Peter. Peter didn't want him to tell me what the meeting was about, but Ryan says that in the car ride on the way to the meeting, which took place on the beach, he said to me, "If you behave yourself, you can get a part in this movie with your dad. Keep your voice low and don't tell him you know about the movie. If you get the part, you don't have to go back to that school."

I wanted clarification. I said, "If I get the part, can I stay with you at the beach?" Ryan said yes. So I followed his instructions, got the part, and moved in with him at his beach house in Malibu, never to return to Tree Haven. Poor Griffin—for a while, he was stuck either at Tree Haven or with my mother.

During the filming of *Paper Moon,* my father and I stayed in side-by-side hotel rooms at the Holiday Inn in Wichita, Kansas. We worked together for fourteen-hour days, and I had the time of my life. It was *Paper Moon* that brought us together and, ultimately, ironically, it would be *Paper Moon* that drove us apart. During the movie Ryan treated me like an adult, although he tried to keep me off the coffee. When I complained that all the actors got to watch the dailies every night, to review what had been shot during the day, my father asked if I could join them. Peter Bogdanovich declined, saying they didn't want me to get self-conscious, but I knew that Ryan was on my side.

In Hays, Kansas, we were shooting a scene in which Addie is waiting for her father by the train tracks. I found a stray cat on the tracks. I brought it back to the hotel, named it Alio (like an alley cat), and semi-trained it to go to the bathroom in the hotel bathtub. Every day I brought Alio to the set. We always had a full car: my on-set guardian, Diane; my tutor, Betty, and her husband, Greg; and Joe, my father's stunt double (who had once gone to prison for kidnapping Frank Sinatra Jr.). Invariably, the cat would defecate in the car. All the grown-ups would make a fuss, but my dad paid them no mind. He let me keep my ill-trained pet and bring it home with me to Malibu.

Ryan recalls that at the start of filming I stumbled over my lines, but by the end, if I made a mistake, I'd say, "Don't cut. Give me the cue. I'll do it again." He remembers that time with pride—watching the actor in me emerge.

Ryan explains my ongoing movie career as the result of purely mercenary motives on my part. He remembers my saying, "You know what I'm going to do with my sixty thousand dollars from *Paper Moon*? I'm going to raise Thoroughbred horses."

Ryan said, "No, honey, not *sixty* thousand dollars. You were paid *sixteen* thousand dollars. You won't get a horse for that."

I said, "But I won an Academy Award."

He explained, "You don't have any money. Really. I do. I got 10 percent. But you don't make money on the first movie. For your first movie you get paid the minimum, scale wages. It's the second movie that makes you money."

There was a silence. Then I said, "Well, maybe I'd better do a second."

In those days, there weren't many movies with parts for children. But an opportunity emerged around Christmas of 1974, right after *Paper Moon* was released. Ryan and I were at a party together, because we went everywhere together. There Ryan ran into some producer from Paramount with whom he had a beef. The producer had called him a prick over the phone. Now, in front of me, they sort of pushed each other. The producer spilled his drink on me, and I kicked him in the shin. Ryan says he and I were like two Gestapo agents shoving the poor guy around.

The next day, the producer called Ryan. Before Ryan could apologize, the producer said, "No, I'm calling to apologize. Also, I have a script."

Ryan said, "What is the role? A German SS officer?"

The producer said, "No, not for you. For Tatum." The movie was called *Bad News Bears*. The role was a Little League pitcher, and this time, since it was my second movie, Ryan was determined to get me a good deal. The producers made a first offer of $150,000. Ryan turned it down. He flatly turned down every subsequent offer the producers made until they got to $350,000 and a percentage of the gross profits. It was a major deal, but the whole thing hinged on whether I could pitch.

Ryan and I played a lot of Frisbee on the beach. I could throw a Frisbee sixty yards, but we had never played baseball. So Ryan got me a glove and we threw ball after ball as he tried to teach me how to rotate my shoulder. The big test was going to be at a park at the base of Coldwater Canyon. A bunch of Paramount executives were going to show up in their suits and ties to watch me attempt to throw a baseball.

The day before my tryout, we went over to Peter Bogdanovich's house. Peter showed me a series of small motions that a pitcher would go through—but not the ones you would expect. He didn't show me how to wind up and throw. He showed me how the pitcher would look at the catcher and shake off his signal. But the batter would be watching, he told me, so I had to shake off the catcher's signal without changing my expression. Once I had that down, Peter handed me a piece of gum and told me to do it again. Chew gum, shake off the signal, no expression, now agree with the catcher without showing the batter. The next day, the tryout was a piece of cake. My throw was no good—it soared out onto Coldwater Canyon, but I looked exactly like a Little League pitcher. The deal was done.

Of course it wasn't the case, but at the time it felt like I was the only child actor in Hollywood. I was certainly the only one at all the grown-up parties. I started dressing up, becoming a mini-starlet. When I did *The Cher Show,* the costume designer Bob Mackie made me a silver gown to wear when I imitated Cher. The show let me keep it, and I wore it out on the town with my beloved platform heels. When I went to the premiere for *Tommy,* the movie based on the album by the Who, the press said that in my sequined gown and heels I looked a little too mature for an eleven-year-old. But I was in heaven.

My father was the center of my world. He was physically affec-

tionate, draping his arm around me, holding my hand. He was loving and nurturing, and I ate it up. For the first time in my life, I felt
truly safe and like I belonged. That gift didn't last forever, but a little
goes a long way. From it I grew enough baby roots to survive.

It is the father I met then—or the security that came with him—
that I longed to have back. That fresh stream in a desert, assuring
me, when I was so thirsty, that there was a reason for me to be alive.

IN SPITE OF our years of conflict, my father had also sort of saved me
once as an adult. After the tragedy of 9/11, I couldn't take the fighting with my ex-husband anymore. I was losing my battle with him,
and, not coincidentally, losing the battle with my own addiction at
the same time. It was lose-lose. I fled New York, missed my drug test,
and in doing so relinquished custody of the kids to John. This was
a devastating blow to my soul and spirit. I wanted desperately to die
and only survived because of divine grace.

In L.A. in 2001, my life spiraled out of control. I was moving
from hotel to hotel, using drugs, before I rented a house in Venice.
And there, I lost it. The doctors call it cocaine-induced psychosis,
but in layman's terms, I was just plain out of my mind. I became
convinced that people were trying to break into the house. I had
locks installed all over, inside and outside all the doors and windows, locking myself in and out. Then I had all the locks changed.
Finally, the day came when I called the police on myself, convinced
that someone had broken in through the windows and was about
to get me.

When the police showed up, they saw the state I was in—clearly
not healthy. They wanted to bring me in on a violation called a 51/50,

which is a code meaning someone is potentially a danger to herself or others. The cops offered to call a family member first—they were willing to release me to someone who would take care of me. I gave them my father's number. I don't know how I still had that number—probably from Griffin. When they called my father, he said, "She can come home to my house." My dad was there for me. He had a home for me.

The police helped me to a taxi. I fell asleep on the way to my dad's. I was exhausted after not sleeping for five nights. When I rolled out of the car into the beach house, I was pretty wrecked. The veins in my arms had collapsed and were inflamed. I probably weighed ninety pounds. Things could not have been worse. I was literally dying.

My father was shocked to see my condition. I think he was slightly afraid of me. But he took me in, and I was grateful. I'd been on my own for so many years that I'd forgotten or doubted that there was someone I could turn to, someone who would care for me no matter how low I'd sunk. *Oh right, I have a dad. I can call someone. I do have a house I grew up in.* That time, my father was there for me. Once again, he saved me.

I CALLED MY father from the parking lot of Whole Foods because at last I felt ready to reconcile the savior my father sometimes was with the man who incited my rage and disappointment. I wanted to rediscover the charming man I'd once known. I wanted to focus on the father who had sometimes been there for me, not the one who usually hadn't. The *Paper Moon* Ryan. If what Sean was experiencing was real, Ryan seemed ready. I wanted to believe that my father was good. He didn't have to be perfect. He was funny and charming enough to get away with a lot less than perfect. More than anything, I hoped we O'Neals could be a family again, whatever the heck that meant.

My father returned my call. Through Sean, we made plans for all three of us to meet for lunch at a little Greek restaurant called Tony Trattoria near Ryan's beach house in Malibu. Three generations of O'Neals, together at last. I wondered if the restaurant needed a permit from the city for that.

A few days later, as I left my new apartment in West Hollywood to head toward lunch in Malibu, I was running a little late. All I could think about was how awkward and scary it used to be years ago when I arrived late to meet my father. He would be outside Farrah's house, busying himself by watering the plants, but always waiting, and when I drove up, he'd shout, "You're fucking late." I prayed that it wouldn't be like that now, or worse.

I pulled up to the valet, gave my car to the attendant, took a deep breath, and walked into the restaurant with my head down. Tony, the owner of the restaurant, led me toward a back table, and there he was. Him. Ryan. Dad. He gave me a huge beautiful smile and opened his big arms. It was just amazing to see him. He looked so handsome and seemed so well. I ran over, wrapped my arms around him and hugged him for a long time. I smelled the cologne he's worn since I was a little girl, and my heart just felt like it took a different type of beat—one it hadn't taken in some twenty-five years. I felt like I was home. I was whole. It was a dream come true.

Sean was there, sitting next to my father. He rose to greet me, and I gave him a big hug. Sean is six foot three, with unruly brown hair, freckles, white skin, and blue, blue, blue eyes. He has his father's physique, but he looks a lot like my father. Sean—my brave boy, the conduit who facilitated this scary reunion. I was so grateful to him for this moment. Three generations of O'Neals. And nobody was getting arrested. That alone was cause for celebration. Cake, please!

Eating lunch with my father and son was surreal. We didn't address the years of absence head-on, and I never expected to. That definitely wasn't my dad's style. He doesn't like to get to the heart of matters unless it's on his terms. He talked about Farrah mostly. The loss was still fresh—she'd died just a month earlier—and her memory was comfortable ground for him. She had loved him unconditionally for years and years.

Later, we said good-bye outside. He gave me a kiss. We promised each other we'd get together again soon.

On the way home, I had butterflies in my stomach. What was I getting myself into? Was it the right decision? Would it pan out, or would I end up wondering why I ever went down this road?

Back in my apartment, I lay down and wondered what the future would hold. Reconnecting with my dad felt incredible. By now the butterflies were mostly gone, and there was a comfort in my chest, like a warm blanket settling over me that said I was home. I had my daddy back.

Or did I?

CHAPTER SIX

THE NEW O'NEALS

SOON AFTER THAT first reunion lunch at Tony Trattoria, I had my third neck surgery in July 2009, and I went to stay at Ryan's beach house to recuperate. The house is huge and impeccably clean. The bedroom I was given was cushy, with a comfortable bed, lots of space, and its own bathroom. The sea air made me feel like I was recovering faster. It appeared to be a perfect environment for healing.

Everything went swimmingly until my housekeeper, who was helping out, tried to defrost the freezer of the refrigerator in Ryan's bedroom. When my father walked into his room, he found water streaming across the floor. Ryan called for me, and when I came to his doorway, I saw him standing in a puddle. Ryan was mad. He said, "That's my freezer, my private place, my area. Why don't you have her clean your freezer? Keep her at your house. This is my place, where I live, Tatum." I kind of yelled back. I said, "Come on, Dad. It's just a freezer."

I'd just had neurosurgery. I was wearing a neck brace. If ever there was an appropriate time to be mad at me, especially for my housekeeper's defrosting skills (or lack thereof), this was not it. As he vented, I felt a painful tingling up and down my torso, which I would later find out was shingles, activated by stress.

I'd been feeling strong and independent, and already he was getting to me. I realized I had to protect myself, take care of *me*. I packed up my stuff, wrote a note saying, "Bye, Dad. I love you," and left.

Ryan apologized and sent flowers. I called him. We were both still committed to preserving the ground we'd gained, so we swept the incident under the rug. But I finished my recuperation at my own home, in my own space.

WHEN SEAN GRADUATED from Occidental in the spring of 2010, he moved in with my father. At first, I was a little apprehensive. However, I hoped and trusted that Ryan would rise to the occasion. Sean's lease was up, and he loved the beach, the sound of the ocean, the sunsets. He is my most poetic child. That year after you graduate college is always tricky (not that I would know). Even more so if you want to be an actor. What better place for Sean to live while he figured out his next move? After all, my dad was an established actor, which was what Sean aspired to. Ryan was happiest when he was working, and he was busy shooting episodes of the TV dramas *Bones* and *90210*. I hoped this might inspire Sean in his career. And, by all accounts, Sean and Ryan were having fun, going to dinners and beach parties, getting along well.

As spring turned into summer, I traveled back and forth to New York to shoot the finale of *Rescue Me*. In L.A., I was practicing my lines for an independent movie—another indie (I had five in the can, waiting for release). A movie I'd shot the previous year, *The Runaways,* starring Kristen Stewart, Dakota Fanning, and Michael Shannon, was opening at the ArcLight in Hollywood, and we all went to that together: me, Sean, and Ryan.

I went out to the beach house on weekends to visit Ryan and Sean. The Malibu beach house, where I'd spent much of my childhood, had gone through major changes over the years. There had been a great pool table. And, of course, this was where I learned to pitch for *Bad News Bears* and to ride horses for *International Velvet*. Factor in the Frisbee games with Ryan and I was a little like those girls in the olden days who could play the spinet, stitch samplers, and not much else. In that house, I excelled at recreation.

At some point, my dad and Farrah had renovated the whole house, and it was transformed into a very special place, with simple, clean furniture, orchids in bloom, and big picture windows looking out at the sea. That summer, it was a wonderful, calm setting, and I spent lots of my free time there.

Ryan and I read lines together, and he helped me a lot. We read my part over and over. He said he wasn't hearing something, though he didn't know exactly what he was looking for. He said, "Deepen your voice. Speak with authority, Tatum." Finally, I lowered my voice and found a certain toughness for the character. He said, "That's it. You found it. Now I can let you go," and released me to go work on the lines by myself.

We weren't all work and no play. Sean and my father played Frisbee and paddleball every day. Ryan and I took walks on the beach

and let my dog, Pickle, run up and down the shoreline. It was nice. I
was reminded of the funny, familiar, everyday details of my father's
life. He exercised every day, then took a sauna. He is the neatest person in the world and super well-groomed. He always smells great,
and his hair is always perfect. Whenever he passed a mirror, he'd
stop, fix his hair, and shadowbox at his image. So handsome! It
cracked me up.

We went to Nobu for sushi, Tony Trattoria, or had mellow cook-
outs at home. Sometimes I'd cook . . . badly. I am capable of cooking
well but, weirdly, not for Ryan. Maybe it's because my dad's house is
a freaking bachelor pad. There are no ingredients to speak of. So I
made the most of spaghetti and marinara. In the evenings I'd ride
his stationary bike while we watched movies and sports together. For
some reason I find documentaries about murder, death, and serial
killers to be perversely relaxing, so I'd hop on the bike and my father
would turn on the Investigation Discovery channel to find *Dr. G:
Medical Examiner.* Then my dad would massage my shoulders and
tell me funny stories about him and Farrah, like the time they were
on the beach and thought a bunch of paparazzi were coming straight
for them. They were kind of excited at the attention, he said, embel-
lishing how they preened for their big-picture moment, but at the
last second, the herd of paparazzi swerved and passed by, revealing
their true target farther down the beach: Paris Hilton. As Ryan told
it, he and Farrah both sat there in stunned disbelief, saying, "Who's
she? What does she have on us? We're Ryan and Farrah!"

Days and weeks went by, and there was no further sign of the
man who had lashed out at me when the housekeeper defrosted
the freezer. When I visited, we laughed often, about everything.
I loved the way, whenever he greeted anyone, even an old friend,

he'd shake their hands and say, "How do you do? Ryan O'Neal: *Love Story*" or "Ryan O'Neal: *Peyton Place*" or "Ryan O'Neal: Tatum's father."

When my dad came over to my house, he teased me about how hard it was to park in my neighborhood—West Hollywood. "It's okay, Tatum, I parked in Palm Springs." It always made me laugh. He had pretty much adopted my cat, Wallis, and they had a speaking relationship. He liked to joke about how the cat was more respectful about getting on his bed. Little, silly things. He was so funny. I loved being around him. It wasn't the stereotypical "perfect family" of a sitcom, but it was, finally, perfect for me.

A CLOSE, STABLE family was something I wanted for as far back as I could remember. When my ex-husband and I were together, we built our unique version of a close family. We always brought all the kids with us when we traveled. Christmases we spent home in New York with a big tree, lots of presents, and a feast with ham, turkey, sweet potatoes, mashed potatoes, string beans, and stuffing—all recipes I'd learned from my mother and John's mother. Those holidays were a new experience for me. I had a window into what having a big, happy family might be like. It was the first time I'd felt any real sense of family . . . and still I couldn't stay.

John and I were so young when we married—I was just twenty-two and he twenty-seven. There were ups and downs. We both brought our own issues to the marriage, and mine were more obvious, but what brought them all to the surface was the fading of his career. After having an amazing year in 1984, John lost his number-one ranking. Around the time Kevin was born in 1986, John took a six-month sabbatical. When he rejoined the tour, he had a hard time facing the young power hitters Ivan Lendl, Boris Becker, and the up-and-comers who had adopted their new style of playing. John's ranking started to slip. He was in his late twenties, which for tennis was a reasonable age to begin declining, but what professional athlete who has been at the top his entire life is prepared to start losing? I felt that he was blaming me for the end of his streak. I understand it better now—that kind of adjustment has to be horrendous for a world champion.

From what I see and hear of him now, my ex-husband is a different person from the one I knew. He's nice, gentle, caring. But at the time there was so much tension between us. Perhaps it wasn't fair to John that I'd gone through so much before our marriage. We were young; we had little kids; we traveled constantly. It was a lot of pressure and I just couldn't hack it.

When I left John, I knew I was dissolving the family dynamic that had meant so much to me, but I had no idea how hard it would be to live alone and to raise kids by myself. The years that followed were the hardest, and the only ways I found to face my own darkness were illegal and destructive.

By 2010, in my forties, clean and sober, I noticed for the first time that I still longed for that big, happy family. I even questioned my decision to leave, especially after watching John get married again and reinvent the family life we might have had together. Had I made a mistake in sacrificing that? I myself was hesitant to remarry, partly because I wasn't sure I wanted to go that route again, and partly because I didn't want my kids to have to get to know someone else. I had always felt displaced by my parents' companions. And hadn't I put my children through enough already?

My children were out of the nest, and for now, at least, I was not trying to replicate that traditional family structure. But the moments Sean and I spent with Ryan, in the place that had once been my home, were happier than I had imagined possible. Life could not have been better. A brief golden age with the perpetual golden boy.

THEN, ONE NIGHT in July, Ryan and I went to dinner with my then-agent, at an Italian restaurant. While we were chatting, my father abruptly turned to my agent and said, "You want to represent me?"

My agent said, "Sure." Suddenly, he was representing my father, too. Didn't that muddy the waters a bit? I sat there, thinking, *What about good old Tatum? Sitting right here at the table. Anybody want to run this by me? Boundaries, anyone?*

As we ate, my—our—agent said, "You guys have a good rapport." He started asking if we'd want to work together, and if so, on what? In the past, I had had the idea of doing a reality show by myself, but by the time we were done with our entrées, we were all caught up in the notion of Ryan and I doing a reality show in tandem.

I wanted to be in front of a camera again. Just before my marriage, I'd begun taking acting classes, wanting to reinvent my image and to be taken seriously. But then John came along. During the years of my marriage, the only role I played was that of a supportive wife and mother. Then there was the divorce, and the tough years that followed. With the exception of some indie movies, there had been a twenty-year gap in my career. I was particularly proud of the work I'd done in recent years. I had stayed with *Rescue Me* for six years. But I never stopped feeling like I had to prove myself extra-hard. *Paper Moon* had been a free ticket for me, an entrée into a career I was too young to know I wanted. Winning an Academy Award at nine years old had put me in an odd position—and I'd spent a lifetime living up to it. I was totally proud of the Oscar—but it was a little challenging to have begun my career at the pinnacle of success and then to realize that I would have to work my way up the ladder again. But I was willing to pay my dues.

My arrest gave me the opposite sort of notoriety. It was a badge of dishonor that I wanted to overcome. I did the court-ordered rehab—two eight-hour class sessions about drugs and alcohol—which cleared the charges from my record. But as far as the press was concerned, I had been convicted.

The notion of a reality show promised not only work but a chance to show who I really was—not the precocious child star, not the out-of-control tabloid headline, but a real, strong, independent woman.

In the next few days, I talked to my kids about the possibility of doing a TV show—a documentary series that followed my life. I'd been offered a few such shows in the past, and they weren't opposed to the genre. But when they heard my dad was involved, they didn't know exactly how to respond. This was a gray area—it was unclear to all of us if it would be good or bad for me. So while they were generally apprehensive, they trusted me and believed in me. They knew I'd make the right choices along the way. They just wanted me to keep them informed. They wanted updates and downloads.

It was talking to my friend Kyle that got me most excited about the prospect of doing a show with my father. He said, "Yay, Tatey! This will be good for you. It's brave to take on something so personal and heart-driven as this." Kyle's enthusiasm was contagious. But as a die-hard fan of *Dancing with the Stars* and *The Real Housewives of Beverly Hills,* Kyle cautioned me, too. He said, "Be careful. I know how sensitive you are. I want you to have a good outcome with your dad, but don't do anything that might be damaging to your sobriety or yourself." For the most part, Kyle was just plain enthusiastic, except that it broke his heart that if the show did go forward, it would take place in L.A. We wouldn't be in the same city, and he wouldn't be able to color my hair for it!

Now that my father and I were a family again, would we really have a chance to work together again, too? I didn't have to wait long to find out. Within days of that dinner with my agent, Ryan and I had meetings with several different production companies. It was on. It happened so fast I couldn't help wondering if my agent had planned it all in advance and maneuvered things so we would believe it was merely a spontaneous inspiration. No matter. The Hollywood train had left the station and we were on board.

CHAPTER SEVEN

THE STORM AFTER THE CALM

DURING JUNE AND July, Ryan and I spent a lot of time together at the beach house and had meetings about the show. We were getting reacquainted. Spending so much time together, my father and I didn't suddenly develop the ability to talk openly about our thoughts or feelings. We certainly didn't talk about the past or attempt to resolve any of our issues. We were both much older than the last time we'd had any kind of relationship, and it felt as though, with Sean as a connector, we were slowly, carefully forging a new family dynamic.

In August, Sean left the beach house to spend six weeks in Ireland as part of a theater group. One day, he was walking along a moor, and he climbed into a tree—presumably, to have a poetic moment, my whimsical child. Somehow, he fell out of the tree and tore a tendon. When he returned to Malibu, he was still recuperating and could no longer play Frisbee on the beach with Ryan. It should have been only a minor shift in the beach-house routine, but it seemed to throw my father off in a bigger way.

It became hard to tell what exactly was going on with Ryan and Sean. They started teasing each other in a not-quite-friendly fashion. Ryan chided Sean for forgetting to close up the Jacuzzi. "Why can't he shut the lid?" he would mutter. Then he'd complain that Sean stayed in the bath or Jacuzzi for too long. Sean imitated my dad saying "Goddammit" in a gruff, angry voice. And Ryan caricatured Sean's long arms, dangling them from his shoulders as he walked. Then Ryan started being curt with Sean, yelling, "Don't do that!" Or, when Sean was wearing his headphones, Ryan would say, "What's he doing in there alone listening to music all day?"

Then my father closed his door. His upstairs bedroom is the gathering place in that house, where we all hung out to watch TV and eat dinner off trays. Now Ryan shut the door. If Sean knocked, he shouted "yes" from behind the door in a tone that said, *Don't bother me.* When they crossed paths, Ryan looked at Sean in a way that wasn't exactly loving. I can't really explain the shift. Was it frustration? Was it simply challenging for a man set in his ways to have a young man around? Was he irritated that his Frisbee partner couldn't pal around with him like he used to? The sun was setting on our Malibu summer.

Ryan probably wasn't even aware that his behavior toward his grandson had changed. I only know that Sean and I felt it severely.

Sean is a pure soul, a sensitive boy. I saw that even when he was little. Before Emily was born, when it was just the two boys, I decided that my second son needed a little one-on-one time with his parents. Kevin, the oldest, was an easy child, and always seemed settled and comfortable wherever he was. Sean was throwing tantrums, fighting to be heard and seen, as second children sometimes do.

We usually took both, and later all the children, when we traveled for John's tournaments, but when Sean was four, I decided it might help him if we took just him to Wimbledon in the summer of 1991. He would have alone time with both parents—well, mostly me while John practiced and played the tournament. So five-year-old Kevin stayed at our Malibu house with the nanny, attending a summer program, while Sean and I wandered around London, going to Hyde Park to feed the ducks, building sand castles, counting double-decker buses. I had been right—all Sean wanted was to be numero uno for a little while. In that environment, without his older brother, he was a perfect joy. There were no tantrums. He was a cheerful little engine of a kid, ready for any and every adventure. This was exactly what he needed.

One day, when we were in a pharmacy, the bobbies came in chasing a burglar, nightsticks drawn. Sean screamed, "Mommy, Mommy! They're going to hurt the guy." I comforted him and tried to distract him as they carried the man out of the pharmacy, but he was deeply worried about the burglar. He was the same way about homeless people in New York. He always wanted to stop and give them money. He couldn't understand why their lives had to be that way. Sweet Sean.

I thought about that sensitive boy in the hands of my dad. I couldn't stop worrying that any one of the traumas I had suffered would befall him. My God. He was not a hardened, wild child like my brothers and I had been. I was only spending weekends at the beach house, and I grew anxious about leaving Sean there with Ryan for the remainder of the week. If anything happened to him, how could I live with myself? I started trying to convince Sean that he needed to move out.

"I'm not liking this. I want you out of there" became my every-day mantra.

It was naive, but when Ryan and I made amends, I really wanted to believe that we could never be angry at each other again. Our relationship seemed entirely different and better than when I was a little girl. So many years had gone by without my dad. How could I have been apart from him all this time? I had missed so much. Now that we had found our peace, I thought it could and would never end. The fairy-tale ending was within our reach and I assumed we both wanted it more than anything.

I should have known. Why didn't I know? If I hadn't been swept up in the fantasy, I would have admitted to myself that underneath it all, things really hadn't changed.

Now Ryan was going after Sean. I was much better at seeing reality when it involved my children. I lifted up the proverbial rug to see what else Ryan and I had swept under there. Weren't we sidestepping the past at every corner? At one point, he said, "I'm reading my journals. I really wasn't that bad. I took you to the doctor." My book *A Paper Life*, which damned his parenting, was the 900-pound gorilla in the room (or, to mix metaphors, the 900-pound metaphoric gorilla "hidden" under that metaphoric rug). From his telling me that he had taken me to the doctor, I inferred that Ryan was defending his behavior in the past and denying all I'd written about it in the book, but neither of us was really ready or willing to come straight out and talk about it. He had his own reasons; I was simply terrified to go there and jeopardize our new, fragile peace.

Sean and I conferred about Ryan's mood. The grumbling to himself. The closed door to his room. He seemed frustrated with Sean, or frustrated in general. We observed the change, but there was nothing concrete to address: no actual conflict, no argument to resolve. Besides, I didn't exactly dive into confrontation with my father. So we did nothing.

CHAPTER EIGHT

DOWN TO THE WIRE

DESPITE THE SHADOWY backdrop of unresolved conflict, Ryan and I had now settled on a production company, Endemol, for our documentary-style series. If we sold the show to a network, Endemol would be the company to put it together, doing all the planning, shooting, editing, and production of the final product. We all agreed that it wasn't going to be a reality show. I see reality TV as titillating drama that is created for an audience. With the infusion of plenty of alcohol, reality TV shows feature women fighting, women wearing couture and fighting, and women with money fighting. Our series would be different. It would show our real lives. It would be the authentic investigation of a father-daughter relationship. Instead of calling it a reality show, we referred to it as a docuseries. I liked the sound of that. The first step toward selling the show to a network was shooting a "sizzle reel"—a short sample video that gave a glimpse of who we were and what the show would be.

We filmed the reel over two days in September at my dad's house. In the days leading up to the shoot, my dad and I were both antsy. Two months had passed since we first had the idea. At first Ryan was raring to go and wanted to start shooting right away. As the days rolled by, I saw his initial enthusiasm waning. In the days leading up to shooting the sizzle reel, he hurt his back, and I worried that it would all fall apart, but the night before the shoot, Ryan was in a good mood, happy and laughing, and I had high hopes for the coming days.

The next morning was overcast and cool. Around ten A.M., the crew, producers, and others started arriving at the Malibu house. Ryan emerged from his bedroom half an hour later. He made a grand, Norma Desmond–style entrance, which he timed carefully, making sure everyone was assembled downstairs and waiting before he descended the staircase. Later he would explain that he did this as a joke that nobody got. I asked him how his back was, and he said he didn't feel great and hadn't slept well. I was nervous because I could tell he was nervous.

They taped the whole day, shooting footage of the two of us playing Frisbee, walking on the beach, sitting on a couch in my dad's living room talking. My father kept saying that everything was great. To hear it, the past was but a distant memory. Our relationship was sunshine and roses. My dad kept saying, "I lost her once; I'm never going to lose her again." But I felt like it wasn't real. The sunshine and roses weren't exactly the whole picture. Wasn't the point of the show to reconcile? And didn't reconciliation start with confrontation? At some point, we had to start talking about what had happened.

The producers were trying to understand what had caused the

rift between us. What, they kept asking, had made the fissure so longstanding and painful? Finally, Ryan said, "I left Tatum for Farrah. That's the rub." The producers then spent the next six hours asking us every question there was to ask. I tried to offer long, thorough answers to what were pretty tough questions. Then Ryan broke in and said, "Oh yeah, also the fact that I wasn't invited to your wedding, and I was virtually abandoned by you." I started explaining to Ryan that at the time I had no control—that John didn't like him, that I was pregnant and felt mentally beaten down by John, and that I knew that no one tells John McEnroe what to do, especially his pregnant twenty-two-year-old fiancée.

Ryan accused me of never inviting him and Farrah to John's tennis matches. "When you did come," I said, "you left in the second match of the second round." I explained that, as far as John was concerned, if you were a family member and you were there to watch him play, you had better watch the first match all the way through to the end of the tournament. John felt that it brought him bad luck if a family member left during a match, which my dad did during the U.S. Open, the first time he went to see John play. Afterward, my dad offered some lame reason that he had to go do something in Los Angeles. Whether or not that was true, John was so angry with my dad that he never invited him back to another match, which I now tried to explain to Ryan.

Plus, I reminded him, that was more than twenty-five years ago! I got very emotional and started crying. The last thing I expected was for *him* to lay into *me* about the past. Was this what he was holding on to after all these years? Inside, I was saying, *What about me? Do you have any idea what it was like for me?*

For the shoot, the crew had arranged the cameras in the ground-floor entrance hall, outside my old room. To access an outlet, the production team moved a couch. There, behind the couch, looped around the banister, was an old, forgotten wire bike chain. Halfway through the day, when I noticed it, a chill ran through me. I knew exactly why that wire was in that odd place, although I couldn't believe my incredibly neat father had never noticed and removed it. This hallway had once been a crime scene, and the wire was evidence of the damage done.

In 2007, Griffin had called me in New York and given me alarming news. He said that Redmond had been shooting up. Our half-brother Redmond—we'd always loved him and worried about him—was flirting with death. Griffin was driving a used cop car at the time, and maybe the cop car was infused with a justice-enforcing pheromone or something, because Griffin said, "I have a great idea. I'm going to handcuff Redmond to the bed for twenty-four hours so he can kick heroin."

I knew this was not a good idea. In fact, it was by far the dumbest idea I'd ever heard. I'd been a hard-core junkie in the nineties, and I was pretty confident that handcuffing a person to a bed was not only a bad approach to most everyday situations, it was also not an effective way to detox anyone. I knew Red would become super-agitated, and then God only knows what he'd do. I said to Griffin, "Dude, I really don't think you should do that."

Griffin didn't listen. Determined to carry out his preposterous plan, he went to the beach house with his wife, Jojo, who was eight months pregnant, to "keep an eye on Redmond" while Ryan went out for the evening to celebrate Farrah's sixty-first birthday.

Ryan says that when he arrived home from a beautiful night out, he was confronted with the scene of his oldest son, Griffin, sitting in a chair in the hall outside Redmond's room—my old room. Griffin had taken the bedroom door off its hinges as part of a complex system he'd rigged to restrain Redmond. Now, standing at the bottom of the stairwell, I looked over at that door. It had long been rehung, looking like a normal door in a pretty house, but I still felt like it was hiding its haunted truth, the ghostly shadows of that not-so-long-ago night.

That night, my father came in, saw Griffin and his contraption, and then saw his youngest son, Redmond, shackled on the floor of his room with a long wire attached to his neck on one end and the other end attached to the banister in the hall. True to his plan, Griffin had tied Redmond up to force him to detox. Using a bike lock.

Ryan shouted, "What the fuck is going on? What are you doing? Unlock him immediately." Griffin refused. Ryan lunged at Griffin. Griffin, convinced he was the only person who would and could save Redmond, grabbed a fire poker and started beating Ryan with it, hitting him over and over. As Ryan tells it, he shouted, "I'm going to be in *Bones*. Don't hit my face," which to me is the only remotely comical part of the otherwise grim story.

Somehow poor Jojo got involved, probably trying to calm things down. But in the melee, she got hit in the face with the poker, and her eye started to swell and bleed.

My dad ran up the stairs and got his gun. My father had always owned a gun. I'd played with it when I was a kid, and once Griffin, at five years old, got into Dad's bullets, throwing them into the fireplace and watching them ricochet around the room. But I'd never seen Ryan himself take it out or known him to use it.

Ryan fired a warning shot. Ryan says that he intentionally missed Griffin, that he fired the shot to scare Griffin off, but Griffin ran to the phone, called 911 (the best decision anyone made that night), and told the dispatcher that Ryan O'Neal was shooting at him and that he needed help. Moments later, the cops showed up and took my dad away. Griffin didn't get arrested, just my dad. Maybe Griffin's used police car bought him credibility. What a sad, ugly night!

The wire now coiled at my feet represented all the misplaced love and violence that clashed that night. It was the sad symbol of an unmanageable life. Gunfights and drugs and chains. *Why was my family doing this to one another? A lot of pain and misery, and for what? Why was there violence and anger where there should have been nurturing and love? We just wanted to survive, me and my brothers. What had we done that was so bad? Why did we have to be born, really? Why was I here? For everything to be destroyed around me? Where was the love that people are supposed to have for one another?*

As Ryan was being taken away, he says he saw Griffin standing in the doorway of the house. In Ryan's memory, which seemed to find the cinematic resonance in any story, Griffin, like a big-screen villain, hurled the poker into the bushes and stood on the threshold to watch Ryan go, arms crossed, victorious.

As far as I know, after Ryan was taken away, Griffin drove Jojo to the hospital. She had almost lost an eye. Later, Griffin would try to press charges on Ryan for her injury, but it was unclear who exactly hit her, so the case was dropped. As for Redmond, he was left in the house, no longer bound but all alone at the grim scene of the crime.

Soon after the fight Griffin called me. He said, "Dude, something bad happened. Dad just got taken away in a police car. He was trying to kill me with his gun."

I said, "Oh my God." After he told me the rest of the story, I said, "I told you not to do that," and it felt like a meager, ordinary response given the extraordinary circumstances, as if I were saying, "I told you not to let the dog out of the house." What else could I say? There were no words for the shame and devastation. And yet, in a way, I was used to this kind of bad surprise. My mother had constantly threatened to kill herself. I was somewhat numb to such news. And I didn't quite realize how bad the situation had been until I saw it on the news. Ryan had been arrested. It was a big, ugly scene. I had to call my children and tell them, and as I did, I knew my ex-husband was sitting there, shaking his head, saying, *I could have told you this would happen.*

Griffin and I had been through a lot in our lives. I love him unconditionally, and I'll love him forever. Our lives—mine, Griffin's, Patrick's, and Redmond's—were a minefield, so full of anger and fighting. Although Griffin's good intentions are hard to pull out of that screwed-up scenario, what I will always understand is that our lives were not exactly fair. And now here I was, filming this relatively peppy sizzle reel with my father for a docuseries. How real was it going to get?

FIVE WEEKS LATER, Endemol e-mailed me a finished edit of the sizzle reel. The narrator's calm, resonant voice intoned, "Meet the O'Neals . . . Like all families, they have issues." I had to admit that it looked interesting. Wouldn't want to live it (though I had and was), and it was a little hokey, but it made for good TV and I was going with it.

Now we had to pitch it.

CHAPTER NINE

COLD FEET

THE PERCEPTION MAY have been that I was a child star who stopped working when I got married, but the truth was that lately I'd been working steadily. I had no doubt that more dramatic roles would come my way, but visibility was definitely a factor in my decision to do the TV show with Ryan. I wanted the acting work to keep coming.

In my life, I'd known the greatest possible range of fortune. I started off dirt-poor in my mother's house, which was in a constant state of disrepair and where I was haphazardly clothed and fed. Then, at six, I moved into the fancy Malibu house with my movie-star dad. By eight, I was earning my own money (which I wouldn't control until I was eighteen). At eleven, I was the highest-paid child actor ever, earning $350,000 for *Bad News Bears*. By fifteen, I had my own credit cards. Nobody oversaw what I bought. Whatever I charged, the accountant just took out of my savings. Cher was my idol, and I developed an obsession with shoes and clothes. I had three of everything I owned, just like Cher. When I was a teenager, Ryan arranged for me to be financially responsible for my mother. I became my mother's parent.

Then, at twenty-two, I was engaged, and in the next several years I had three kids with John, who had more money than I had ever had. There were private planes and homes everywhere. I was constantly remodeling houses. That became my hobby. That's what rich people do. I guess my understanding of money went a bit haywire, because all of a sudden there was just so much of it. It kind of lost its meaning to me. As I transformed into the wife of a very wealthy person, my identity was corrupted by the assumption that with great wealth comes happiness, which, as it turns out, it *does not*. Money can keep you distracted from looking at the big picture but not forever.

When I left my marriage in 1993, I left John's fortune behind. What money there was in the divorce settlement I spent almost carelessly, as if I wanted to use it up quickly because it was tied to the past, to a relationship gone sour. It wasn't given willingly, and I never felt like it was truly mine. In the years that followed, I was not nearly as financially comfortable as I had been at various times in my life or might be again, but what mattered most was that I was free.

After September 11, I had lost custody of my children, and I left for Los Angeles because I thought I needed to give up, that I was a true failure as a mom, an actress, and a woman. Around that time a significant amount of money went missing from my account. My accountant at the time kept telling me it was my fault, that I was spending too much. I knew that wasn't the case, but when I pressed for answers, he scolded me for accusing the company of mishandling my money. Isn't there always one of these accountants in a story like mine? I allowed myself to feel ashamed. If I'd been sober, I definitely would have figured out that something was seriously wrong and that it wasn't me. I left that accounting firm because I knew in my gut that the whole company was a crooked mess. It was an instinct, and my instincts have often served me well. Soon afterward, I read in the paper that the head of my former accounting company, Ken Starr, had been arrested for stealing $30 million of his clients' money in a Ponzi scheme over the last few years. Had I been more aware, had I not been using and dealing with the emotional wreckage of my past, I would have caught on to what that firm was doing far earlier.

Time passed. I spent ten years litigating over my divorce and my kids, and have since gone through many periods of feeling poor and worrying about money, working hard to make ends meet and to take care of my children.

I'm not opposed to a fancy life. I had one, and it wasn't bad at all. My ex-husband and I lived in one of the biggest apartments in New York. We had serious houses in Malibu and Long Island. When we went to Paris, we stayed at the Bristol. He bought me expensive jewelry that I have locked in a safe-deposit box to some day give to Emily. A girl can get used to that kind of life.

Having been there, however, I can now say without reservation that I don't need to be rich and I don't need a rich man. I've loved being humbled the way I have, because I'm happier now than I was when I had money and whatever I wanted. Being rich makes many things look easy, but, as I said, it just doesn't guarantee happiness. In the beautiful Upper West Side apartment I shared with John, I watched the world passing me by. I felt like Rapunzel, trapped in my tower. I just wasn't happy. I wanted and needed out.

Now, sixteen years after my divorce settlement, I earned my own keep, and for the past ten years I had lived on what I earned. I helped my children financially. But there were plenty of middle-age actresses without drug histories. It was too easy for Hollywood to write me off. That reality motivated me to do everything I could to make the most of career opportunities.

I had thought long and hard about doing the TV show. Now it was rolling forward, and I was optimistic. Endemol set up meetings for us with several cable networks. Ryan started off willing and chipper. He'd switched from introducing himself as "Ryan O'Neal: *Love Story*" to "Reality Ryan."

I did all of the talking in the meetings. I'd say, "This is the story of a reunion. A father and daughter who had a great relationship that was torn apart by their careers, their dynamic, and their personal struggles. It's about a woman's struggle to find what's left of her family." I explained that we didn't know what might come out on-camera—we weren't perfect, by any means, but we had a lot of ideas and were willing to explore our relationship in different ways.

Those meetings made me proud of how far I'd come. After all, I hadn't picked acting as a career. It had picked me when I was too young to know myself. I was just a ranch kid, a wild child, and I didn't arrive in Hollywood with enough confidence or fortitude to carry me through a whole career. I could barely speak in public. Then, when I was nineteen, just before I met John, I decided that I wanted to be an adult actor, but I wanted to do it right. I didn't have any formal training, and I couldn't rely on my childhood aptitude growing with me, so I went to New York and enrolled in acting classes. From then on, for the entire time I was in New York, I took acting classes off and on, whenever I could. Even when I was primarily focused on being John's wife, I always knew I wanted to better myself, to perfect my craft.

Ultimately, I took the same approach with life: I hadn't been given the basic life tools to develop into a strong, self-confident woman, so I worked hard to become the person I wanted to be. I spent years in AA and years in therapy. I searched inside myself. It was hard, but it was worth it.

At last, I was in a position to show off the results of my years of hard work. I was finally capable of making eye contact without feeling the urge to bow my head like a naughty schoolboy awaiting punishment. Finding grace and dignity in those meetings was a real achievement for me.

As we went to the first few meetings, Ryan was enthusiastic, but soon, when we had our postmortem chats, he started to voice some doubts. Would this ruin his film career? His chances at an Oscar? I was pretty sure he was joking about the Oscar but not entirely. The upshot was that my father was hesitant about what this kind of exposure might mean for his career. And, truth to tell, so was I. I believed in the show, felt that it could bring about much positive change for me, my dad, and perhaps even for viewers. Nonetheless, if not done well, our good intentions could backfire. Long story short: we didn't want to be turned into laughingstocks. My old friend and former agent Sue Mengers is a Hollywood legend. I'd met Jon Hamm at one of her parties and, out of the blue, he said, "Don't you ever dare do a reality show. You can't." Ha! Easy for him to say. I do like to think of myself as a legitimate actress and I thought our show was different, but I didn't know how it would be perceived. What about my career? My pedigree? But I wanted to make my decision based on the work before me, not on the fear of industry perception. I believed in this show.

For all the potential pitfalls of exposing one's real self on television, I thought we had a rare chance to make something quirky and different and dark and funny. Ours was a story people might relate to: a parent and a child reconnecting after many years of estrangement. And I couldn't help hoping that if our reunion played out on the screen, where Ryan was so comfortable and proud, maybe it would buttress our relationship. Maybe it would be the mirror he needed to face his own past, present, and future. Maybe it would help our newfound fledgling family dynamic endure.

From the beginning Ryan's mood was unpredictable. At one of the production meetings—before we found Endemol—there was a glass of water waiting on the table in front of his chair. Ryan arrived a little late and everyone else—producers and some executives from a cable network—was already in their seats. When Ryan sat down in his chair, somehow he was hunched over in such a way that he smashed his forehead into the glass. Blood poured down his face. That's right—head hit glass. It was a dramatic and seemingly impossible feat of coordination. Before I could reach to help him, he turned toward me and said, "Did you put that glass there?" He later would joke that, in his mind, I shifted the glass just before he made his entrance, that it was all a plot.

I made light of it: "Dad, stop sitting down headfirst."

The table of executives chuckled, and Ryan joined in: "Do I have to do this in every meeting?" We never did manage to reenact how his head was so low and yet so . . . forceful. I was scared that he would be too embarrassed to show up at another meeting.

We had first started thinking about doing a show in July. Now it was September and Ryan's attitude toward the show darkened. After three months of being on board, Ryan started threatening to quit. I was pretty frustrated—I'd made this commitment and I was ready to go through with it. Every time Ryan threatened to quit the project, he had his reasons, though they weren't the reasons one might imagine. For instance, if I missed one of his phone calls, he threatened to quit. Missing Ryan's calls was different from missing Emily's calls. Emily and I had an arrangement: if I missed one of her calls, I would call her back as soon as I was able. I understood and respected her concern for my well-being. Ryan and I were two adults, yet he expected me to answer my phone—at all times—not because he worried but because he wanted me to be immediately available whenever he wanted to talk to me. Could I be in a relationship with someone who expected me to answer the phone whenever he called—even when I was asleep or in the shower? *Answer your phone!* I had no idea how to react. *Answer your phone!* How could I have a normal conversation after that? Finally, I stood up for myself. "I can't always answer the phone, Dad. Sometimes I'm busy. People don't always answer their phones."

Then, for fear Ryan would quit, I called and texted, apologizing, and trying to woo him back. Wasn't I a fool, to put myself in a position where Ryan had the power to disappoint me over and over again?

Then we met with OWN, Oprah's new cable network. The morning of the meeting, I put on gray jeans, high-heeled black booties, a black silk shirt, and a leather jacket. I wore my usual makeup, but punched it up a little with some bright red lipstick. I got my hair done, so it was sleek and flowy. I was trying to be glamorous. From the minute we walked in, it was clear that this was a network that wouldn't sensationalize, manipulate, or exploit us. At OWN, we'd found our home. We sold the show. Now came the tricky part—making it.

CHAPTER TEN
HOW CAN YOU DO THIS TO ME?

WE DIDN'T EXACTLY celebrate making the deal with Endemol to produce the show for OWN. The process of bringing the show from concept to reality had taken far longer than Ryan and I had expected. In my dad's life, everything needs to happen fast, and he still seemed frustrated at the pace. And, as I found myself jumping through more and different hoops, I realized I had to fire my agent. Ryan and I were trying to iron out our separate agreements with the various players, and it became clear that sharing a representative created a conflict of interest. There was quite enough conflict in the equation already, and I bowed out. That also meant that Ryan couldn't instruct me to contact our once-mutual agent with his questions or ideas; if he had something to say to his agent, it was now up to him to do it.

Putting our negotiations aside, for Sean's twenty-third birthday in September I planned a family celebration at Matsuhisa, our favorite sushi restaurant in West Hollywood. My father and Sean came together, arriving a little late. They joined Sean's stepsister Ruby (John's wife Patty's daughter) and her friend; Sean's best friend, Doug; Ryan's friend Marketa; and me at the table.

I was expecting a nice evening, but as soon as Sean came in, I thought he looked agitated. My father, too. I was worried. *What was going on? Was Sean okay?* I must have given Sean some kind of questioning look, because suddenly he said, "Don't look at me like that. Don't look at me like that."

He went outside and sat on a bench. I had no idea what he was talking about. It wasn't ordinary for a glance of mine to freak Sean out. I followed him outside and sat beside him. He said, "You can't look at me like that—you're condemning me. How can you do this to me on my birthday?"

Those words, coming from Sean, were familiar, though the last time he'd said them had been in much worse circumstances—five years earlier, on one of my worst days as an alcoholic. Right before *A Paper Life* was published in 2004, I was living at the Mercer Hotel in the heart of SoHo. I wasn't using drugs but I was still angry and willful. I was complying with the judge's orders for regular drug testing, motivated by my desire to be with my children. But simply complying with the court system isn't an indication of the highest level of sobriety. The system doesn't necessarily lead to true sobriety. I hadn't yet made the spiritual shift.

Although I wasn't fully aware of it at the time, I was still trying to get away with whatever I could get away with. I was more interested in fighting John and the system than looking at my problems and dealing with them directly. I knew that alcohol wouldn't show up in the court-mandated tests for drugs in my urine, and so I decided that it was fine for me to drink occasionally. I'd never been anything but a social drinker. That soon changed. Quick riddle: What do you call a junkie who takes up social drinking? Answer: An alcoholic. There followed a three-month drinking period that was anything but social. I remember drinking sixteen mini-bottles of vodka, throwing them into the trash one after another. *Bing,* each went as it landed in the can. *Bing. Bing. Bing.* At some point during my stay at the Mercer, the housekeeper stopped refilling the mini-fridge with mini-bottles. She said, "Oh no, Miss O'Neal, we can't put more in your room." Yep, as it turned out, I couldn't drink, either. Alcohol: not good.

In 2005, Sean's eighteenth birthday came around. He was staying on the couch of my room at the Mercer, and I came home drunk. He said, "How dare you do this to me on my birthday?"

And now he was asking me that question again. Hearing those same words five years later, I was taken aback. I didn't know what I'd done, but I knew I hadn't violated his trust this time. In fact, ever since his eighteenth birthday, I had tried to make every one of his birthdays as loving and wonderful as possible. It's one of the ways I make my living amends to Sean.

On the bench outside Matsuhisa, Sean told me that he felt like I was scrutinizing him. Later he would explain to me that it was because things were tense at the beach house with my father. But in the moment, I just apologized for probing and coaxed him back into the restaurant.

Eventually, my father paid the check and we all said good-bye. The night hadn't gone smoothly—the unresolved issues among us were bubbling just beneath the surface—but we'd gotten through it without disaster. Or so I thought.

My apartment was pretty near the restaurant. Within minutes of my arrival home, my phone was ringing. It was Sean. He said, "Grandpa kicked me out of the car. Can you come get me?" Sean was stranded on La Cienega Boulevard, not far from the restaurant. I ran downstairs to get my car.

I was livid. The last thing I wanted, especially on Sean's birthday, was for him to experience anything like I had experienced as a child. I wasn't going to hold my tongue just because we had some TV deal. I called my father and said, "You promised. You promised you would not attack or hurt my son! You are a monster and I hate you!" The past slammed into the present, and out spilled years of pent-up rage. He couldn't get away with this. Not anymore.

"I hate you," I screamed. "You and your fucking gross problems."

Before he could respond, I hung up the phone, so angry I couldn't stop shaking. Ryan had already threatened to quit the show over much smaller issues. I knew he would quit for real this time. Well, so be it. No TV show was worth the destruction to my family and me. I'd come to him—and to the project—determined to love him until he could love himself, but as it turned out, that was easier said than done. It was over. We were over. All that work and effort— it had been thrown out on La Cienega with his grandson.

Twenty minutes later, Sean and I arrived back at my apartment and talked about what had happened. Sean and my father have plenty in common. Sean is careful and methodical. He keeps his stuff neat, just like Ryan. They both like sports. They were a good roommate match for a while. But the moodiness I had witnessed in my father had gotten worse since I had left the beach house. There wasn't any-thing Sean could do right. Sean felt as though he was trying to stay out of Ryan's way, but no matter what, he was still underfoot. Perhaps this was why I sensed they were both edgy when they arrived at the restaurant.

According to Sean, the fight was triggered by a discussion Sean, his stepsister Ruby, and I had at dinner about the fact that Sean didn't want to appear on the upcoming TV show. Sean felt that the show should be about me and my father; it was, after all, subtitled "Ryan and Tatum." It was our business, our relationship, not his. I understood that and had no need to bring him into it. But, for whatever reason, Ryan seemed to take Sean's decision as a rejection. At the time, this was the only explanation I could come up with. In any case, Ryan had overheard Ruby, Sean, and me talking. He waited until Sean got in the car, then turned around and said, "Tell me right now you're not going to be in the show."

Sean said, "I'm not going to be in the show, Grandpa."

Ryan said, "Get out of my car." This baffled me. Why did Ryan need Sean to participate? What did it mean to him that Sean chose not to? Why had Ryan thrown Sean out of the car? As far as I was concerned, people don't leave their grandchildren in the middle of La Cienega Boulevard. Period.

As predicted, soon after I yelled at him on the phone, Ryan sent me a text saying to tell the people at Endemol that he had quit the show. I texted back, "If you want to quit, please do it yourself."

CHAPTER ELEVEN

CAUSE AND EFFECT

WITHIN A FEW days I found Sean an apartment a couple of blocks from mine. I was relieved that he was finally out of Ryan's house, but devastated that everything we'd worked for had fallen apart. We hadn't even begun filming, and the show had already changed every-thing. This wasn't *Paper Moon*—we weren't a movie star in his prime and an eight-year-old girl who hung on his every word. The show was about us, as flawed adults, and it forced all of our issues to the surface in an unnatural way. It made Ryan tense and uncertain, so he lashed out at Sean. It weakened me, because now we shared a commitment. The show was a documentary but was already affecting how we lived. Was it all a huge mistake?

Was Ryan capable of being the father I longed for? Did he even want that role? Was it just another role? Was the problem the TV show, or was it us? Which was damaging the other? Which mattered more? It was tough to separate the two. In a way, I wanted the cameras to bear witness to our behavior. I wanted a connection with Ryan. I wasn't ready to let go of any of my goals. But there was nothing I could do now. It appeared to be over. I wasn't ready to contact Ryan, and all was silent from his end.

In the past, a situation like this—my father and son fighting, my father and I not talking, the show we'd worked on close to collapse—would have given me a reason to check out. I didn't like feeling helpless. I didn't like waiting for people to come through for me. Being able to trust—it's a work in progress.

But now I had an army of support. I went to meetings frequently and regularly. People would notice if I missed them. My sponsor, Patty, is my fortress of strength. She has the empathy of a saint, and the insight to pinpoint what kind of support I need and when I need it. She is a constant in my life.

Although Patty's sobriety is natural for her now, after twenty-five years, she sometimes has her own issues—the problems that arise in a sober life—that we talk about. She had a breakup that we went through together. Her stepfather had recently died. While she had stayed with him in the hospice, the tables had been turned, and I was grateful for the opportunity to be there for her. I listened to her and what she was going through. I loved to remind her how good she is to people, how she is a strong influence with real purpose in the world. I didn't need to talk about myself all the time. Sure, I was fighting a bit with Ryan, but I was okay. Above all, I never stopped appreciating the commitment Patty had made to me. Despite her full-time job, she always found time for me. I relished any chance to pay her back.

I was driving home from a meeting when I told Patty about the fight on Sean's birthday. I was frustrated at the situation. I couldn't bear not knowing what would happen with the show. I said, "I don't like the way it is. I don't want it to be like this. I want life to be different. I don't want to always be fighting."

Patty said, "Take a deep breath and know that you are supposed to be here. Go home and pray for your dad."

I said, "I don't want to fucking pray. I'm trying to do everything right." I hung up the phone.

As soon as I hung up, I regretted it. I was still upset, but at the same time I was terrified at how Patty might respond. What if she was angry, what if she stopped speaking to me, what if I lost her? I called her back right away—five seconds after I hung up. "I apologize," I said. "I was being petulant and difficult and a total brat."

She said, "It's fine, Little T." That's what she calls me—her Little T. I knew we were cool.

Patty and I talked through the fight, and, with her help, I saw that my reaction had been overblown for the circumstances. I thought my anger was noble: I wouldn't let Ryan mistreat my son. But the more Patty and I talked about what had happened, the more ambiguous it seemed. I didn't understand kicking a kid out of a car and I'd gone into Mama Bear mode to protect my son. I lashed out defensively. On the other hand, come to think of it, I had once on a trip to Montauk pulled the car over to the side of the road and told then-sixteen-year-old Sean to get out and walk. I guess grandpas can get mad, too. (Of course, I picked Sean up after he'd walked a little bit. That's where my father and I differ.) I'd said hurtful things to Ryan without ever giving him a chance to say his piece. I told him I hated him. Why would he want to do a TV show with me if I really hated him? I regretted saying that to Ryan. I had lost control, just like he had. I did to him exactly what I had been asking him for years not to do to me. So no one wins. Instead of the thoughtful, measured, adult approach that I wanted to bring to my relationship with Ryan, I had brought my fury about the past to the present situation, a big bundle of pent-up anger that wasn't going anywhere fast.

This was a revelation for me. If Ryan and I were ever to truly reconcile, I had to stop playing my role in the unproductive drama we'd enacted over and over for so many years. I had to break my part in the patterns of behavior that had misguided us most of our lives. I decided to make the first move toward peace.

I sent Ryan a message saying that even if we didn't do a show, I would still be his daughter and I loved him. He texted back the next day. It was brief: "Tate I am going to see Oprah with Ali and we'll talk next week." He and Ali McGraw were due to appear on *Oprah* in honor of the fortieth anniversary of their movie, *Love Story*.

Then, a few days later, another text came from Ryan. In it, he mentioned that he had sent a text to Sean. He continued in his standard, well-suited ALL CAPS: "WALLY [that's my cat who was still at Ryan's] IS NEXT TO ME, BUT SEAN HAS DISAPPEARED BUT NOT SO MUCH AS A GOODBYE GRANDPA. OH WELL EASY COME EASY GO." He signed off with "LOVE YOU." It broke my heart to read that message, which spoke volumes to me. He clearly missed Sean but had no idea how to fix what had happened. There was love between them, I believed that, but it was stifled by the barrier they themselves had made. And so the sad history of Ryan and Tatum was repeating itself with the next generation.

My dad may have truly believed that he didn't do anything wrong or hurtful, but like it or not, Ryan is a parental figure for Sean.

My dad doesn't process feelings like most people. Instead, he gets aggressive and, when I was a kid, that led to some scary moments. I never stopped worrying about how it might play out with Sean. I had hoped Ryan had turned over a new leaf, but there was no guarantee.

Sean didn't reply to Ryan's text. He probably understood my father well enough to know there wouldn't be an easy or thoughtful resolution. Time would tell.

UNLIKE FOR SEAN, it never took much from Ryan to soften me. We both wanted to put the fight behind us. It belonged in the past. I wrote him back: "I will watch *Oprah*. Love you." I didn't mention Sean. That was between them. But I felt his sadness and hoped that Ryan could redeem himself. I knew he had it in him. His warmth is a greater force than his temper. A little of his love goes a long way. All the light that I have today came from a few critical years of his affection.

Later, when I congratulated Ryan on his *Oprah* appearance, he forwarded me the text message he had sent to Sean. In it he apologized and said he was sad, and he wished Sean luck. I was moved and impressed to see that Ryan had expressed his regret. It was a big step for him to take, and it was a step in the direction I hoped everything would go—with him and Sean, with him and me. It gave me real hope for our family. At the same time, I wanted to set clear boundaries. I wasn't going to get in the middle of Ryan and Sean's relationship. I wrote to Ryan, "I don't know what you want me to say."

He wrote back: "T, I just thought you should know that he blew me off. He never responded. Be good to each other." There were a few ways I could read that, but the simplest interpretation was that he wanted a relationship with Sean, he felt he had tried, and now he was giving up. I felt sad to think that both of them would let go so quickly, but only the two of them knew exactly what had happened between them, and each of them knew how much it was worth to himself.

Meanwhile, as the third point of this dysfunctional triangle, I still had no idea whether Ryan was back on the show, or if he'd even officially quit to anybody but me. Time passed, and I tried to be patient. I tried to observe my impatience. I tried to be patient with my impatience. Patty told me that I was powerless and this was God's plan. She reminded me that rejection is God's protection. But all the 12-step rhetoric still wasn't sitting well with me. I just wanted to hear, "Don't worry. If you stay sober, everything you want will happen for you." And even more than wanting to hear it, I wanted to live it.

Eventually I came around to Patty's way of seeing things. I'd gone through enough and come so far. I trusted in God, and believed that He didn't let me take those meetings, pitch and sell the show, get so far with Ryan, just to have it all disappear. Every daughter needs her father. I had faith that it would work out, and I held on to that rather than despair.

Originally, Ryan had invited me to move in with him. We thought spending time in close quarters would help us connect. With the help of Patty and other friends, I decided that no matter what happened with the show, I would not move into the beach house. Not with my anger ready to explode at any provocation. The nonexistent, tenuous show was changing before it had even begun.

CHAPTER TWELVE

TWO NIGHTS

WHILE I WAS nervously waiting to hear what was happening with the show, I was invited to a party at Sue Mengers's house. The last time I'd gone to a party at Sue's, I'd been underdressed. L.A. is the land of jeans. Dress 'em up. Dress 'em down. You can get away with the right jeans anywhere from Spago to a premiere. So I had walked into Sue's wearing my usual: skinny jeans, boots, and a leather jacket. The way the memory plays in my brain, the entire room turned to look at me, thinking, *She's in fucking jeans?* Among the guests were Lorne Michaels, Jon Hamm, Tom Cruise, Brad Grey, Jennifer Lopez. On second thought, they probably weren't too worried about my jeans or anything about me. Anyway, Sue was always looking out for me and she must have been remembering that over-casual night when, before the party, she said, "Look as good as you always do, but don't forget it's for John Clark." ("John" is not his real name, but John was a major Hollywood mogul, and this party was in his honor.) I got the point. No jeans this time.

Sue Mengers is widely known as the first female super-agent, and she was my agent from when I was a child through age seventeen. She throws the quintessential Hollywood party in her fabulous Bel Air house. I've been attending her parties since I was nine, and met everyone there at one time or another. At one of Sue's parties when I was twelve, I fell in love with Dustin Hoffman and wrote a song for him. I've met Woody Allen, Robert De Niro, Michael Caine, Elizabeth Taylor, Gore Vidal, Warren Beatty, Robert Redford, Paul Newman, Candice Bergen, Ali McGraw, Diane von Furstenberg, Barry Diller, and every other star of the seventies and the eighties.

Sue's parties were always an exciting prospect, and I was looking forward to this one, but I have general discomfort at Hollywood parties. Plus, I had almost always gone to Sue's parties with my father, but my dad and Sue had had a falling-out, so now it was just me. I may be on some "Hollywood Royalty" party lists, but I still feel like Little Tatum from the ranch.

The night before the party, I tried on outfits in front of Pickle. I settled on black shorts, black tights, a black jacket, a black T-shirt, and heels. It looked like my usual uniform, minus the jeans.

I parked in Sue's circular driveway, and the butler opened the gigantic door. Sue was holding court in a stylish French chair. She was wearing a long, loose dress, with her beautiful hair cascading down. Sue is as maternal toward me as a take-no-prisoners woman like Sue can be. When I arrived a little after eight o'clock, I found out that Sue, as usual, had asked me to arrive at eight and everyone else to come at seven thirty. I guess Sue likes me to make an entrance.

That night, in Sue's grand living room, there were a variety of powerful, interesting people assembled, including Eva Mendes, who had big hair, big rings, a dress that looked like it was Yves Saint Laurent, a fur-trimmed jacket, and the most awesome huge boots with twelve-inch heels and zippers up the sides. Fabulous.

Food was eaten. Jokes were made. To Sue's delight, John Clark seemed to like me. I felt good about how I looked and how the night was going. Then the conversation turned in a way that threw me off-guard. Some of the executives started talking about what certain top actors were getting paid. One TV actor was making $40 million a year on a sitcom. Another was at $10 million. They were boasting about the big salaries they were paying these actors, and I felt sick to my stomach.

It was a little past midnight. I don't know where people may have thought I was going, but I slipped out the front door and left without saying good-bye.

I might be too sensitive for these Hollywood parties. Now that I'm sober, there are a lot of times I still feel uncomfortable in my own skin. Like I really don't belong.

Later, after sneaking out of Sue's party, I told Sean what had happened. "I just left without saying good-bye. I don't know if they noticed." I had felt so completely invisible. Sean reminded me that it is not normal for people to earn $40 million a year. It's not normal or particularly classy to talk about them. Why was that a topic of interest or conversation? Didn't people have better things to talk about? Sean had a point. But I knew the reason I was self-conscious. I take everything so personally—something to work on.

As for my hostess, I knew Sue would forgive my early departure. She always says, "Honey, with the way you were raised, I'm surprised you're not selling yourself on the corner of Hollywood Boulevard with a needle hanging out of your arm." (Funny, though, I haven't been invited back since I made my covert exit. So it goes.)

THERE'S A REASON I didn't end up where Sue envisions me, and it is a combination of my own will and the 12-step program that saved me and continues to help me survive. The morning after Sue's party, I got up at six thirty A.M., walked Pickle, then went to the seven thirty A.M. AA meeting that I usually attend. Sometimes, when I want to feel glamorous, I put on makeup before I go, but that morning, I just pulled my hair back, stuck a baseball cap on my head, and slipped into the room, which was slowly filling with people. As much as I care about my appearance, meetings are not about being seen. I know it is important to be able to go into those meetings, as tired and needy as I might be, without caring what people think. The point is to be there, however you are, to strip oneself of ego and vanity, and to get better. As they say, you cannot save your ass and your face at the same time.

In contrast to Hollywood parties, like the one at Sue's, my meetings are a social world in which I am instantly comfortable. When I entered the room that morning, I was met by the familiar smell of coffee—the stale breath of the abstinent alcoholic that makes me feel like I am home. I recognized most of the attendees, as I always do, even as the faces rotate throughout the week. I picked a chair near the front to make sure I could hear the speaker without being distracted by the stragglers.

As I started concentrating on the prayers and readings, a warm feeling flooded over me. When the speaker began, I was fully transported into another alcoholic's life. It helped me forget myself and the self-doubts I was carrying from Sue Mengers's party the night before into the day ahead. The truth is, it doesn't matter how much money you have if you have some peace of mind.

Almost every day I go to a meeting to sit, listen, and share. I love hearing the intense story of what each person's life was like before he started using, what happened when he met drugs and/or alcohol, and what his life is like now.

Some of the speakers had loving parents and stable families. Some, like me, did not. All of us experimented with alcohol and/or drugs and, for some reason, spun out of control. There are all sorts of stories from all walks of life, but after hearing many of them, day after day, I now see the common threads of damage, pain, survival, and hope that weave through them all. Every one of us has found a way to live without the dread and self-loathing that are the biggest challenge to recovery. It can be very hard to drag yourself to meetings, make friends, and believe there is a reason to go on. It is a tremendous gift to hear how other people fought their way back, and how they found a way to live happy, healthy lives. As I listen, I feel love for the speaker—even if I don't foresee wanting to forge a friendship. I love him for making it to that podium.

Above all else in that room is the love that helps people survive. The support group promises to love you until you can love yourself. That amazing, unconditional love is palpable in the room.

Individually, the stories are deeply inspirational. There's a man who goes to one of my meetings—let's call him Bob—who is a true success story. After getting sober at the age of thirty-eight and starting with nothing, he created his own real-estate business and is now worth millions. His story inspires me, because when you're addicted to drugs and/or alcohol, you're so broken and bruised that the idea of getting sober is hard enough to imagine, let alone going on to launch a hugely successful business or career. It all seems so out of reach when you're using. I felt very differently about Bob's hard-won fortune than I had about the shallow talk of TV-star salaries the previous night.

Then there is Mark, a thirty-year-old friend of mine who often sits with me at meetings. One of the achievements of his sober life is that he has become a person who is always there to help someone who's not doing well and needs extra support. One morning, I noticed that Pat, a man whom I usually saw at my seven thirty A.M. meetings, hadn't shown up for the third day in a row. Though he had stayed clean and sober for almost two years, I suspected that Pat was using. After the meeting, Mark and I drove to Pat's house—there's a rule that you're never to go alone on a "sober call," so your own sobriety is not compromised—and we coaxed Pat out to breakfast. We convinced him that he needed to go into treatment, and that day, he checked into a residential treatment center.

Carrie W., who was my original sponsor in L.A., is still one of my good friends. She is smart, funny, and beautiful, and she has been sober for twenty-five years. Every time I hear her story, I am newly inspired.

When it is my turn to talk, I give a relatively unemotional, straightforward account of my history of substance abuse. It goes something like this:

The first time I got drunk was when I was six years old and living at the ranch. At one of my mother's parties, I got into the grown-ups' beer. All I remember is sleeping on the floor in the bathroom (instead of in my bed, which was also in the bathroom). By that age, I had already been sexually molested twice.

I started smoking pot when I was twelve and living with my dad. I was a habitual pot user for three years or so, at which point I started adding other substances, like quaaludes, coke, and alcohol. Before I turned sixteen, I had been molested by two men and two women.

At fifteen, I had the first of my many spiritual awakenings when, under the influence, I was in a car accident in which I was thrown from a Jeep out onto the highway. My leg required two major surgeries. I was so grateful to have survived that in the hospital I swore off all drugs.

When I was eighteen, I started using coke in an effort to lose weight. I continued to use coke until I got pregnant in 1983 at the age of nineteen. I was determined to be a mother who never touched drugs or alcohol.

I stopped everything until 1995, when, in the midst of a horrendous custody battle, someone introduced me to heroin. I used heroin, on and off, through many detoxes and rehabs, until I finally stopped in 1998. I was clean until September 11, 2001, when I fled New York and my custody battle for a freefall back into addiction in Los Angeles.

A year later, I went back to treatment and stayed clean but for my close call with crack in 2008. Luckily, the relapse that I was headed toward was averted by my arrest—so you could say God protected me from that one—or from myself!

My neck started to deteriorate in 2004. Since then, I have had three surgeries. Each time I had minor slips with pain pills, but otherwise, I have been close to 100 percent clean and sober for seven years.

I have been sober since June 29, 2010, because that is the day after I took a pill I didn't need for the arthritis I now have in my neck. It was a single prescription pill, and when I took it I hadn't used illegal drugs for five years, but I count from that pill, because that's how we do it in my 12-step program. Some people treat that date as a critical fact in one's sobriety. I don't see it that way. That small slip, the fact of that date—I see it as a very personal, private matter. But they say you are only as sick as your secrets. So I want to give that date, not because it is so meaningful to me but because I hope that in being open and honest about that moment, that single pill, maybe I will help another person to be honest about the small but significant bumps along the way. There is shame in mistakes, but there is greater pride in honesty. So I have been sober since June 29, 2010. For that, I am proud and grateful.

I spent years poisoning my body to avoid the pain, physical and emotional. What have I learned from it? At first, I had to accept that I lived with a cistern of pain. It was no use to pretend it didn't exist or to cover it up. No quantity of any drug in the world was powerful enough to dull the pain for good. Heck, when I'm in pain there isn't a drug that will abate it for an hour, much less forever. Once I accepted that, I began the ongoing process of dealing with my pain in a healthy way, through words, prayer, exercise, friends, and, of course, my support group.

I LIKE TO start the day by plugging into the bigger purpose of life at a meeting. When you see others fighting for their lives, it puts all your own small daily struggles in perspective.

Sometimes I go to meetings at night, when I'm feeling more social. At nighttime meetings, sometimes I dress up as if I were going out to dinner, to see Patty and other friends, and to find the social exchange that other people might have in a bar or somewhere else where people are drinking. It's nice to be surrounded by nondrinkers. People who have been sober for thirty years are amazingly bright-eyed. They have good color in their faces. It's a look you only find on sober faces.

Going to a meeting was the perfect way to clear my head after Sue's party. My purpose was plain to me. And I was reminded that there was a reason Sue's words about my life on a street corner never came true. Because I was fighting it every step of the way.

CHAPTER THIRTEEN

ON AGAIN

I CHANNELED MY anxiety about my career through my lawyer, Jodi. I was calling and e-mailing her about the situation with the man formerly known as "Reality Ryan." If he didn't do the show, what was our backup plan? Could I carry the show without him? What would it be about? How would we structure it? Jodi counseled me to let go and stand back. She didn't think I should try to woo Ryan back to the show. Very wisely, she noted that if I did that, then when the show began, he could put it all on me. *Tatum, why are the cameras in the house? Tatum, why are there people in the garage?* He could quit an infinite number of times, knowing I would keep running back to him and begging him to reconsider. He needed to return on his own terms, to acknowledge to both of us that he was doing the show of his own will.

Jodi, who is a great advocate for me and other strong women, advised me to establish a new pattern of behavior with Ryan. She said, "Don't sweet-talk this person into something he's already going to do." If I let him take responsibility, she was ready to bet money that he would reappear. But I couldn't see it. In my world, things fall apart. I try to fix them. That's what I do. But I took Jodi's advice. I sat on my hands and tried to distract myself.

Then, after waiting what felt like forever, but which was actually just three weeks, I heard that Ryan was in. Ryan, of his own accord, had called Greg, our producer at Endemol. When I spoke to Greg, he said, in his slow, methodical way, "Your dad said that he's going to do the show." There was no announcement, no apology, no drama, no resolution. Ryan just quietly reappeared. Maybe this was how Ryan apologized. Maybe the act of swallowing his pride, showing up, and moving forward was his way of expressing regret over the quarrel with Sean. Even if he wasn't accepting culpability or apologizing, he was at least indicating that he wanted to let it go. At long last, I was coming to accept this as a kind of resolution.

The show was back on. Great! Or was it great? I had to shift gears. I'd been spiraling around the collapse of the show, and suddenly we were planning the first day of filming. Now that I had the show back, did I still want it? At the end of the day, I still believed that the camera would be our best mediator. As actors, the one thing we cared about most in the world was how we were perceived. If somehow my father gained perspective on our relationship, it would all be worth it. Or would it? It was a gamble.

I was hoping that Ryan's participation meant I was back in his good graces, even though I was the one who had reason to be angry with him for how he'd treated Sean. The last I'd heard from him was our brief exchange after his *Oprah* appearance. There were so many unresolved conflicts. I texted him to say that Endemol wanted to start filming on my birthday, November 5.

Silence.

My father had become an active texter. From the moment he'd started, he never stopped. When there was no response from him, that meant something, but I wasn't sure what exactly. Did it mean that he was annoyed that the start date was centered on me? Or that he didn't like me being the one to give him the information? Or that he just didn't like my birthday? Maybe, it occurred to me, it had been so long since we'd celebrated each other's birthday that he had forgotten when mine was and felt embarrassed.

It was mid-October. When I told Greg that in November I'd be celebrating my forty-seventh birthday at the home of a friend, he said he wanted to start filming that night. A birthday party—a celebratory occasion on neutral turf—that was a perfect way for me and Ryan to try again, this time in front of the cameras. It made sense for who we were and where we were. I was relieved, even excited. The torture of being in limbo was over.

WITH THE START date set, a weight was lifted from my shoulders. I had a job lined up—what better time to see how my daughter was doing at college? I wanted to catch up with her and to meet her new friends, so we planned a girls' weekend. I booked rooms at a nice hotel in San Francisco for Emily, her friends Christina and Claire, and me. Over the weekend I took them for manicures, facials, and massages. We walked around the city. We went out to fancy dinners. It was a very nice time for us.

I was happy to get to know Emily's new college friends and to hear what their lives were like. Even though I was still "the mom," to some extent they included me in the girl talk. It struck me that this was one of the benefits of being a single parent. If I were visiting Emily with John, or another man, would she and her friends still open up and tell me about boys and all the *stuff* that girls talk about? I doubted it.

It was also nice for me to have a window into what it might have been like for me if I'd gone to college. Of course, I'd visited my sons. In fact, I'd seen a little too much of Kevin's dorm room. It was such a mess that, once, he lost his cell phone in it for weeks. Tired of being unable to reach him, I drove up to Skidmore to find it. A sticky layer of peppermint schnapps covered every available surface of Kevin's room, punctuated by coins and cigarette butts. It was disgusting. I sent Kevin away, pulled on rubber gloves, and cleaned the whole room from top to bottom. When I gathered up a pile of clothes that was shoved onto a shelf in his closet, I unearthed his cell phone.

So I knew my way around a dorm room. But experiencing college through my daughter was different. I had a constant feeling of living vicariously. I myself had missed out on school, camp, college, all the youthful experiences where girls build so many interpersonal relationships that it becomes an effortless part of their adult lives. So, like an anthropologist, I observed Emily closely through her high school and college years as she easily and naturally developed strong friendships. To me, college was a wonderful period of growth. How cool to be a young person, learning and playing, with no greater obligations. Without putting pressure on Emily to achieve anything in particular, I felt the glow of the experience she was having.

A couple of days later, I returned from San Francisco to the real world, where I wasn't a carefree eighteen-year-old. I was about to have another birthday, and, if all went well, a nation of viewers (or at least a respectable fraction of them) would tune in to see it.

CHAPTER FOURTEEN

BEAUTIFUL CREATURES

MY BIRTHDAY WAS approaching. I had grown up surrounded by actresses who fought their age with every weapon available to them—plastic surgery, makeup, primping. Where did I stand? Would I—could I—be happy in my own skin at forty-seven?

The first woman I watched deal with aging was my mother, Joanna Moore. My mother was a woman who couldn't have been more beautiful, inside and out, but she had an unimaginably hard life, which I will come to. Though she was always striking, with green eyes and a heart-shaped face, she didn't want to age gracefully. In a desperate effort to stay young and beautiful, she changed a lot about herself, even her name. She wore a wig, fake nails, and false eyelashes. She taped the skin of her face up to her head in a makeshift facelift before she had a real facelift. She wore caftans, heels, multiple necklace strands, and always had a cigarette in one hand

and a drink in the other. With the smoke and perfume, the overall effect wasn't glamorous but quite dramatic. My dad likes to say, "You got your acting talent from your mother. Boy could she act!"

I rarely saw my mother without her wig on, but once Griffin, who liked to make her chase him around, bolted through a first-floor window. As she followed him out, her wig caught on the windowsill and got pulled off. Suddenly my mother was standing on the sidewalk, screaming after Griffin, her wispy real hair enjoying a rare glimpse of sunshine. She could and did laugh at this vision. She could always laugh at herself.

My mother struggled with her inner and outer selves. I always saw her beauty and wish she could have forgiven herself for her substance abuse. I have long forgiven her.

My mom fought aging by transforming herself. Even while she lay in the hospital, dying of lung cancer, she still managed to put on those individual eyelashes every morning. I loved her for doing that.

Farrah became my de facto stepmother when I was fifteen. Her walls were lined with the magazine covers she had graced, forever young, forever perfect. She was an icon until the day she died. I can't imagine what it was like to have been the most famous poster girl on the planet and then to age, surrounded by images of your "perfect" self. But through all of it, including a ravaging early death to cancer, her bravery and beauty shone through.

I was left to find my own way as I tried to age gracefully, and I am still forging my own path as the years pass.

I laughed when my father referred to me as a "chick" in the meeting when we discussed our show with OWN. He said, "I had no idea this chick was so together." I'd been making my own money since I was nine. In reaction to my mother, and in part because she couldn't or wouldn't mother me, I was pretty much a woman by the time I was fifteen. So I thought it was pretty funny when Ryan called me a chick in the meeting.

I see certain actresses at my gym in West Hollywood. They're in their late sixties, and they have long, curly hair and huge fish lips. They are bizarre caricatures of their former selves. I mean, what is the sense in that? What message are we sending our daughters? That getting older means we're no longer beautiful? Too many women in Hollywood are messing with their faces and losing track of what normal looks like. A horrible, expensive, warped new standard of beauty is emerging: The Fishface. I'm not against all the techniques women use to stay young, but I do think a little goes a long way. I have no desire to look like I'm in my thirties as I hit fifty. I've *earned* my age; I'm lucky to be here and I want to celebrate it.

I want to age. I want my daughter to be proud of me, and I use that notion as a guide. My daughter is proud of me if I eat healthy food and live well. In this land of artificial everything, I want to stay real and authentic, true to my heart. I enjoy being a grown woman, and I plan to embrace it as life passes. I don't wear short skirts. I don't keep my hair really long anymore. I don't want my life and work to be dependent on my looking like a twenty-year-old. This doesn't mean I'm prudish or that I don't want to be a sexy woman, but I want to be ladylike . . . or at least to try. So the furthest I go is skinny jeans and high-heeled boots. I don't want to wear the same clothes as my daughter would wear. It's her turn to be the young, sexy one. I don't want my sons to have unrealistic expectations for the women in their lives. True beauty evolves.

. . . .

AGING AS GRACEFULLY as I could meant sailing through my forty-seventh birthday and the party that was now upon me. Easier said than done.

My birthday fell on a Friday. When I woke up that morning, my father and I still hadn't had a real conversation since the night of Sean's birthday. Yes, he had signed on to doing the show, and yes, we'd exchanged a few texts about his appearance on *Oprah* and about Sean, but there hadn't been enough of a conversation to let me know where I stood with him. A couple of weeks before my party, a friend of his had called to tell me that Ryan was going to attend but warned me that he was going to ask, "Why did you do this to me?" or "What did I do to deserve this?" Wow, well, jeez. I didn't want a blowup, and I was hurt, but mostly this forewarning just made me sad.

Then I had a bit of an epiphany. My father and I had achieved a loving, balanced relationship when we reunited after Farrah's death. Why would he risk that? Maybe he had his own doubts and fears. I wanted to sustain the balance that we'd found. I wanted it to serve as a foundation on which to build a solid relationship with Ryan. But if I wanted real change, maybe the best thing to do was to let go of all my preconceptions about how it should be and just wait and see the reality unfold, on-camera and in our lives.

It occurred to me that Ryan might not show up at my birthday celebration that evening. But it almost didn't matter. I love birthday parties. My friends would be there. The show was launching. There was plenty to celebrate.

MY BIRTHDAY MORNING still did not get off to a great start. The phone rang soon after I woke. It was my brother Griffin. I had

With my parents—so much hope and promise.

My favorite picture in the world of my dad and me.

As a baby in Ryan's arms. Our early bond is what pulls us back together.

Farrah, Ryan, Griffin, and me in the 1980s. There were times when all was well. *(Brad Elterman/Getty Images)*

Playing pool with Ryan at the beach house.

Young Tatum, baby Kevin, and young John in happier times—England, c. 1986.
(Dave Hogan/Getty Images)

My mother and my daughter, 1994. I wish we could all
look at this picture together and wonder what was in the sky.

With my three beloved children around 1998. I appreciate every moment with them.

Kevin, Emily, me, and Sean at Kevin's college graduation in 2006.
This is one of my favorite pictures.

With Emily out on the town in New York, 2007. *(Jim Spellman/Getty Images)*

At the 2008 Tribeca Film Festival with Perry Moore (*left*), Emily, and Hunter Hill (*right*)—with no idea Perry wouldn't make it. (*Bryan Bedder/Getty Images*)

With Denis on the last day of shooting the *Rescue Me* finale—what a great experience.

With my dear friend Kyle at the premiere of *Frozen River* in 2008.
(Brad Barket/Getty Images)

Kevin, his girlfriend, Caroline, and their dog, Nate—I call them the three blonds.

With Ryan on our way to the TV Land Awards for a tribute to Farrah, 2010.
(Photograph courtesy of Marketa Janska)

Ryan where he is most comfortable: in his bed with the dog,
surrounded by family photographs.

Ryan and Sean in their honeymoon phase, 2010. *(Photograph courtesy of Marketa Janska)*

At a bowling party with Kevin. Wow is he tall and handsome! *(Sylvain Gaboury/PRPhotos.com)*

On the beach with Ryan at the start of our show, both of us trying to make it work.
(© 2011 Endemol USA, Inc.)

called Griff a week earlier to say happy birthday to him. (We're Irish twins—every year we are the same age for a week.) It had been great to talk to my brother—it always is. But, without thinking it through, I had told him about the TV show that Ryan and I were doing.

Now Griffin was calling me. He wished me happy birthday, but then he started asking difficult questions about the show. He sounded anxious, and I realized I had made a mistake by telling him about it without preparing him. It appeared as though I'd triggered all sorts of bad memories for him. I'd provoked his desire for some kind of resolution without being in a decent position to support him. I felt terrible.

I struggled to explain as best I could how I saw it. "Griffin, Dad isn't likely to address and apologize for everything you remember. We aren't making *that* show. If you want to make a show about retribution, you go ahead and pitch it. But that's not my goal. I'm not going to force Dad to come to terms with anything. This is a journey. I'm trying to find peace with Dad. He's moved on, and you need to do so, too."

Griffin said, "Yeah, he has no remorse, no remorse."

That was the substance of my birthday conversation with Griffin. It was painful.

Griffin is a ruggedly handsome mixture of my mother and father. He has green eyes and freckles and plays the piano and guitar so beautifully, all by ear. He's never had a single music lesson. I love, love, love my brother. When I feel sad and alone, I always know I can turn to Griffin. He can always clarify the truth of our lives, because he was there alongside me.

But Griffin and I have had a tumultuous relationship. We survived together, and for each of us, surviving meant losing pieces of ourselves and living with the scars. Griffin seems trapped in the unpleasant memories of his youth. At the slightest provocation, he tends to rant about what happened to us and how horrible it all was. I can't blame him. I'm not suggesting that he forget any of it, but sometimes it feels like he might be reliving the original trauma with the same depth and agony every time he speaks of it. I wish he didn't have to go through all of that. Griff needs to move on a little, for the sake of all of our kids. But that's easy for me to say. Griffin is charming, sweet, and keeps me in stitches. But he is Ryan's son, and a bit of a loose cannon at times.

BY THE TIME I got off the phone, I was already exhausted. I wanted a different, calmer voice in my ear, and I summoned my own, relatively new inner voice. *Griffin is an adult. He can find his own way. He will be all right, Tatum.*

Then I discovered that while I was on the phone with Griffin, Sean had left me a message. His neighbors in the apartment building were complaining about noise. Sean's apartment had a bare wooden floor and he likes to sing—loudly. Sean has many great qualities, but I guess he got a little carried away with his singing.

I called Sean back to ask, "Why today, Sean? It's my birthday!"

Sean said, "Look, Mom, I spoke to the building manager. I'm allowed to sing during the day. I'm not singing at night. But I'll try to be quieter."

It seemed like a lot was happening in one day. Added to the phone calls of the morning, I was nervous to see my father that night.

. . . .

THE PARTY WENT off without a hitch. I was wary of seeing Ryan, but when he arrived, it was perfect—or as perfect as we O'Neals can get. He just came up to me and said, "Hello, Tatum." I said, "Hello, Dad." We stood there a bit awkwardly. Then he tried to make a joke: "Is there a way to get a drink here?" *Because it was a sober party, get it?* I laughed, and in that moment I could see that there was no cause for worry. Before me was a warm, congenial man who was, to all appearances, happy and proud, if a little uncomfortable about the omnipresent cameras.

At times like these, my fear of my father feels unwarranted. Why did my anticipation of his anger eclipse the real scope of it? Was it because I had been so terrified of losing him when I was a child that I still catered to his whims? Or was it because he had been a different, scarier guy when he was younger? I believed it was both but more the latter. My father has always had a big, booming voice. Much as my father had mellowed, I still saw him as the looming, volatile father I had when I was eleven, and I still reacted to him with the same deferential fear.

The party had been my first real attempt to assemble my L.A. friends. Since leaving New York, I had been making friends at meetings and reconnecting with old friends. It was never easy for me to make friends, and the jury was still out on some of the people I had assembled, but I liked looking around the party and seeing old friends and new. Patty was there, representing the sober, strong women I wanted in my life. Ryan had been a gentleman all night. It had been a long time since I'd spent a birthday with my father, and having him there made my L.A. family complete. I felt healthy and pretty. The food was delicious. Everyone had a good time. The night was wonderful. I felt awkward but okay. I was optimistic. L.A. might work out after all. What's more, I was really happy with the way our first night of shooting footage for the show had gone. I felt so comfortable, I barely noticed the cameras. My father and I were tentative but trying. It felt real. For the first time in my on-camera life, I wasn't playing a character. I was just being me, Tatum.

Being Tatum meant acknowledging that I felt a tangle of thoughts and emotions: worrying about what we were shooting and whether it would feel right; second-guessing what I said and how I looked; wondering what I might be doing to my career; trying to shove pride and ego out of the way and be grateful that I was working at all. There's no question: it was more exhausting to be Tatum than any character I had ever played. But I was happy.

Tonight peace had been made. Tomorrow I would visit my father at the beach house.

CHAPTER FIFTEEN

WILD-GOOSE CHASE

THE NEXT MORNING, I woke up full of doubt. As I thought about our history and the issues that stood between us, I felt proud of myself for continuing this relationship with my father. But the warm, fuzzy feelings of the night before seemed to have sharper edges in the harsh new light of day. Ryan had no real desire to revisit the past and face up to what kind of father he'd been. Hadn't he made that abundantly clear? What could I possibly expect when I saw him at the beach today, and the next time, and the time after that? Why was I trying to pry thoughts, reactions, and emotions from him when they seemingly didn't exist? Wasn't this an exercise in frustration and futility? What was the point?

When I had first called Ryan, after my revelation in the parking lot of Whole Foods, I was open to healing our wounds, but if it didn't happen, I was willing to go on my merry way. Then we put the show together, and it introduced a new factor into the equation. We now had a shared commitment. I needed Ryan to fulfill that commitment. But I didn't want to force us into a relationship just because of that. Nor did I want to force confrontation for the sake of dramatic TV. We were messy enough without cameras. I didn't want to destroy the tentative peace we'd found.

A darkness fell on me. I had lost faith in the reasons I wanted to reunite. I had lost hope in finding something deeper. I couldn't see our future. In my head, we were back at zero, and this would happen again and again.

BY THE TIME I arrived at the beach house, it was late afternoon. I made dinner for Ryan and me. At my birthday party the night before, Ryan had asked why Sean wasn't there. He was shocked when I said it was because of him. During dinner, Ryan brought up Sean's absence again. He was obviously trying to wrap his head around what had gone so terribly wrong between them.

I said, "What did you do to Sean?"

Ryan said, "I threw him out of the car."

"Yeah. It upset him," I said. My father didn't seem to realize his impact on people.

Ryan paused, then he said, "That night, after we left the restaurant, Sean and I were on our way to do karaoke. I had never done karaoke before. But Sean told me he'd decided he wasn't going to be in the show. I was stunned. He said, 'Monty Clift, Brando—they wouldn't have done this.'

"I said, 'True, but you're not them and neither am I.'

"I don't really want my life on film—who does?—I did this to please you, Tatum. I'm a grandfather. The old guy. I thought Sean would be the strapping, handsome boy in the show. We could pass him the ball, and he could carry it."

Ryan continued, "Sean said, 'I want people to see me playing parts. I don't want them to see me as myself.'

"I said, 'We have another motive. To support your mother.' But Sean was adamant. The hair on the back of my neck rose. Sean had been living in my house, in Redmond's room. I'd made adjustments for him. Now he'd made this decision. I pulled over to the side of the road and said, 'Out.'

"Then you called and told me you hated me. I was the guy who was sticking with you, being there for you. If you tell me you hate me, I believe you. I didn't want to work with someone who hates me. But we got past it, and I thought, maybe she doesn't hate me. And here we are."

Ryan and I hadn't done much of this in our lives—going back over a disagreement and explaining our perspectives. Though I still disagreed with what he had done, it was eye-opening. In his version, the behavior that had seemed so abrupt and cruel to me at the time now seemed to come from a place of love for me.

I said, "I don't hate you, Dad." I smiled.

LATER, DRIVING HOME, I thought about what Ryan had said. At last I knew both sides of the story, but my heart was heavy. I wanted Sean to be able to have a relationship with his grandfather.

These two men, my father and my son, were so dear to me. The words, the explanations, were coming too late. All this conflict was for nothing. We were a family, but we had no idea how to make it work. Would we forever be breaking apart and piecing ourselves back together?

Without a doubt, just as my father had his own version of the fight with Sean, he had his own version of my childhood. Surely it, too, was shaped in his memory by love and devotion. I knew that, at some Jurassic level of his conscience, he was aware that all I revealed in *A Paper Life* was true to *my experience*. If he didn't have guilt and regret fossilizing somewhere deep beneath the surface, he wouldn't have showed up at all those meetings for a TV show about our relationship, he wouldn't be inviting me to spend time at the beach house, and we wouldn't be in this awkward situation. If he was capable—on some level—of accepting that my experience was different from his, shouldn't I try to do the same? The core of forgiveness is seeing both sides and, moreover, allowing both versions of an event to coexist. We had to make space for each other. How hard it was, to allow truth to be broad and shadowy and rife with contradictions.

All at once, I saw that there was a reason I'd locked myself into a TV show. Just by nature of spending so much time together, my father and I were having actual, unscripted conflict and resolution. It was uncomfortable for me, but something I realized I needed to do if I wanted to break out of lifelong self-destructive behavioral patterns. When I was young, I was always on the defensive. I felt attacked by everyone. I wasn't reared to challenge my father, as a child or as an adult. And now, I wasn't supposed to bring up the past. I wasn't supposed to tell the truth. On the other hand, to be fair, my father has story after story of how tough it was to raise me on my own. But I wasn't that little girl anymore and he was no longer that man.

My father was older. The loss of Farrah had a profound, life-changing effect on him. Death has a way of putting everything in perspective. He was tired of being angry all the time. He was the same Ryan in many ways, but a softer, kinder vintage. I was a little more brave, and he was more open. Added to those changes, the docuseries had a real purpose. When it came to facing the past, the show forced my hand. Through its lens, I would give him the second chance I believed we both wanted and deserved.

When I got back to my apartment, I called my producer, Greg, and said, "Let's go back." I told him I wanted to return to the beach house to see my father as soon as possible. I felt it was important to keep the momentum going.

Greg said, "Are you suggesting this as a producer or as a daughter? We want you to think like a daughter. How do you, as a daughter, feel about going back there? Are you inspired?"

I thought for a long moment, and said yes. The simplest reason was that Ryan was happy to see me. But the bigger reason was that I had turned a corner. I was ready to dig deeper. If it was at all possible, I wanted to help my father take responsibility for his life. My father thought that life just happened to him. He never felt like he was calling the shots. His children happened to him. My mother fell apart; that happened to him. The ups and downs of his career happened to him. Our show was happening to him. In his mind, all of his behavior was a response to the bad things that happened to him. Consequently, he didn't feel responsible for any of his actions. I understood his fear of exposure in the course of making the show, but I was determined to be gentle and respectful, while urging him to take ownership of his past, present, and future. I had come a long way in the month since Sean's birthday, when I thought my attempt to find a new relationship with Ryan was over. I wanted to go back to the beach house. I wanted to talk. Complacency—acceptance of the status quo—wasn't enough for me.

I texted Ryan and made plans to come, with the cameras, and stay for the whole weekend.

PART II

REGRET AND HOPE

CHAPTER SIXTEEN

THE MAN BEHIND THE CURTAIN

THE NEXT SATURDAY morning at the beach house, the film crew arrived at ten o'clock. I had been awake for a while, but there was no sign of Ryan. An hour passed. I left the cameras behind and went for a walk on the beach, past the actor Stephen Dorff doing push-ups on his deck, all the way to an outcropping of rocks. The beach was as glorious as ever.

It has always been hard for me to have a broad perspective on my life. I was trained to survive the moment. Now I was my own master. I made my own choices. But I still had to wait for my oversleeping father on this windy Malibu morning. When would my life truly be my own? I turned around and headed back to the house, thinking these thoughts.

At the house, Ryan finally emerged from his bedroom. He gestured from the top landing of the stairs for me to come up. I did, and I changed into sweat clothes so I could ride the exercise bike while we talked and the cameras ran.

Today, Ryan was in the mood to read to me from one of his journals. He has journals dating back to the seventies. The part that he read didn't go deep and was his story, not mine. So I cycled in place, going nowhere, listening to Ryan read from his journal and its description of the rosy world that he chose to preserve. We sure remembered things differently—that was clear. When I couldn't take it anymore, I got off the bike and went to get ready for an event that evening. It was a dinner for people who'd donated to Hollywood Arts, an arts academy for at-risk young people. I was scheduled to present an award to Howard Samuels, a friend who is a cofounder and director of the Wonderland Center—a rehab for the stars.

PATTY WAS GOING to the event with me. She came over beforehand and we watched a beautiful sunset over the beach, then headed to Hollywood. The event was being held at Raleigh Studios.

It was a great evening. I felt good in my black dress and makeup. I ran into some old friends, including Farrah's best friend, Alana Stewart. The speech I gave to commend Howard went smoothly. Tom Morello from Rage Against the Machine played. Patty and I had a nice time together—she said I was the best date she'd ever had. Afterward, I dropped Patty off at her house and headed back to Malibu. I was in a great mood now, happy and proud. I liked my friends. I liked my life. And when I got back to the beach house, Ryan and I had plans to watch Manny Pacquiao face off against Antonio Margarito in the World Super Welterweight Championship. My dad is a major boxing fan and has had me watching fights since I was a little kid. This was a big one, and I was looking forward to it.

I walked in, put my stuff down, and headed up to my father's room. He was lying on the bed. Without a hello, he said, "Have you really thought about this therapy thing, Tatum?" I was taken off-guard. Where was he going with this? And now that he was venturing into somewhat rocky terrain, where, oh where, were the cameras?

I said, "I do think we should do therapy, yeah."

He said, "Have you thought about what might come up?" His tone was foreboding, and the implication was that I had deep, dark secrets that would be exposed during our televised therapy sessions.

I said, "I want us to get better, Dad. I'm not afraid of what it's going to bring up for me."

"What about me? There are things I don't want to bring up, Tatum."

I said, "What do you want me to do?"

"I want you to stop it. What about Farrah, shouldn't we protect Farrah?"

I said, "What about me?"

Then, at the top of his lungs, he yelled, "I love you!"

I felt dizzy with fear and anxiety. *This* was the father I had grown up with, the mercurial father who mixed love and anger. My father yelling "I love you" while I sat frozen. That was us in a nutshell. He loved me, but he didn't know how to say it. I was afraid of him, even when he was doing his best to communicate. We were trapped in the pattern we'd developed years ago. We could do better. As an adult, I believed I was capable of breaking my side of the pattern, but it would take some work. Same with my father—I knew he wanted a different dynamic, but he wasn't going to putz around the kitchen and suddenly launch into the reality of what happened.

We needed therapy, the very therapy that had triggered this outburst.

I did feel conflicted about pushing Ryan toward what had the potential to be enlightening but would definitely be painful. I didn't want to hurt him in the twilight of his life. But the worst pain we were talking about facing in therapy was also the truth. As hard as it may be to face, I believe that the truth never does damage. It only heals. But I had no idea whether my father could or would ever see it that way.

CHAPTER SEVENTEEN

BETTER LATE THAN NEVER

NO MATTER HOW old we are, growing up and growing away from a parent takes a major emotional toll. It reverberates throughout our lives. I think that part of why my son Sean first turned to Ryan as a father figure and why he was now leaning on me was that he was going through post-adolescent separation issues with his dad. And, of course, now that he was on the West Coast, where Ryan and I were, and John and Patty lived in New York, it only made sense that Sean would transfer some of his emotional dependence to the nearest adult authority figures—Ryan and me.

Sean is twenty-three. He's a grown-up, but in some ways, still a child. I want him to learn to stand on his own two feet and to be an independent adult, but even so, he needs a parent and, given my absences in years past, I'm grateful to be there for him.

Through a friend, I had helped Sean get a job at a restaurant. At twenty-three, this was to be Sean's first real job. He was going to be a waiter. To me, having a job signified young adulthood, responsibility, and the ordinary experiences of growing up and trying to make a living, which I'd never had. Sean was going to take people's money and give them their change. Radical.

Sean went to the restaurant for a few training sessions. But a couple of weeks later, he said, "I can't do that job. It's not working for me. I am not a restaurant person. I don't care about food. I'm not good with the service industry. I have to find something else to do." He stopped working. He wanted to sing, play music, audition, and look for a job that would work for him. This was his decision, and I let him make it.

As a parent, I don't scream or force opinions on my children. I don't think conflict gets me anywhere. Instead, I try to get to the heart of the matter, all the while thinking about how what I say sounds from my child's perspective. I told Sean, "For me to continue to support you, I need you to have a job and to make some money of your own."

Then I got an angry e-mail from the friend who had helped arrange the job. Sean had still been in training when he left the restaurant, and I had assumed that he left on good terms. According to this e-mail, that was not the case. He had just taken off without notice, leaving the restaurant high and dry. I was shocked and disappointed.

Here I was, trying to see my son through that tough first year after college. I was trying to help him get on his own two feet, so I'd found him a job. Now, it seemed, he hadn't acted responsibly. So much for my efforts.

I said to Sean, "Are you kidding? This is how you leave the job after my hard work? What's up, kid? You tryin' to embarrass me?"

Sean said, "I know, I'm so sorry." I told him to apologize to my friend and to the restaurant manager, explaining why he felt the need to leave, and why he did so without giving proper notice.

Like most mothers, I worry about all of my children pretty consistently. Sean, as the one who wasn't in school or working, was top of the list at the time. It had been more than two years since my arrest, and my children had recognized the change in me. I was solid, and it made them feel safe in a way they never had before. This is a feeling all children should have, and I had wanted to give it to them for years, but it had come a little on the late side. The response was different with each of my children. Sean, in my opinion, was acting out now because, at long last, he didn't have to worry that I'd go back to using. Maybe since I was stable, he was free to take risks.

Sean, as I've said, is a sensitive kid. I was careful with how I parented him. In becoming a parent, I thought often about how I was parented, and I did my best to understand and forgive my mother and father.

There are good reasons my mother, who was a warm, loving soul, ended up the way she did. My mother's parents and sister were killed in a car crash when she was six, leaving her an orphan. She was first adopted by one side of the family, who couldn't afford her. Then she was adopted by the other, wealthier side, but there was no salvation to be found there. Rumors spread that a member of the adoptive family molested her. Still, my mother's beauty and dramatic flair were irrepressible. From a young age, she could sing, dance, and play the piano. She was the life of the party, even before pills and alcohol controlled her. She went to a good college, where she was discovered and brought to Hollywood. In Hollywood, the studio executives introduced her to speed, the de rigueur method of keeping young ingénues slender. Like Judy Garland, Marilyn Monroe, and so many others, my mother became addicted. My mother never talked about the horrors of her childhood. If rumors are true, which they too often are, she, like me, was rescued but ruined by her hero. I understand and forgive her—how could I not? Her heart was true—that shone through. If she hadn't lost her own parents, everything would have been different. Maybe she wouldn't have lost me.

That Tennessee Williams–esque history, the tragic loss of her family, being adopted twice, still being mad at and in love with my father—it all added up to an adulthood of drug and alcohol abuse. I understood this as I got older, but when I was a child, I just wanted her to be my mother. I wanted her to be alive and awake. And, I am somewhat ashamed to admit, I was angry with her for not having a beach house, a Mercedes, and my dad's effortless coolness. I wanted a life where everything was rosy, and I was furious at her for failing me. We fought, often because I would accuse her of being drunk and she would say, "What are you talking about? How dare you, Tatum? You're lying. Goddammit, you're always making up stories about me." Her denial of her alcoholism was almost worse than the alcoholism itself. I smelled it on her breath and knew that she was lying. And, oh, I was so mean. "Pull yourself together," I'd scream at her, at seven years old.

It was always important to me as a parent to draw certain boundaries for my children, no matter what was going on with me. I made sure to look them in the eye and say, "Yes, I have problems. Don't ever think you are a part of them. You're not. This is me. This is not your fault." I always wanted them to know that they didn't cause my problems. It was in my upbringing, my family, my blood.

At the same time as I took responsibility for my struggles, I insisted that the children treat me with the respect that I wish I'd always given my own mother. I would often say, "I hear some resentment in your voice. What's the issue? Let's talk about it."

In contrast to my mother's youth, to all appearances, my father had a golden childhood. His parents—my grandparents—were, to my young eyes, a beautiful, loving couple. My grandmother had long strawberry-blond hair that she always kept in a bun, a smooth face powdered to be pale and perfect, full red-lipsticked lips, and dark eyebrows. She was always elegant, wearing nice pantsuits, white or beige gloves, and Rive Gauche perfume. She had a British accent—we're not exactly sure where it came from—and was always saying "Dahling Tatum." My paternal grandmother was the only woman who was a constant in my life and who, at times, bathed me, fed me, and nurtured me. How I miss my "Mummy" now—her softness and warmth. I loved her so.

Ryan was always handsome and charming. Once, when I asked him, "How come you're so funny?" he said something like, "Because I never thought I was very smart. I had to rely on something else to get the girl. I thought being funny would do the trick." My father has always wanted the girl, and he has always gotten her!

My grandma was an actress, my grandpa a successful screenwriter. They produced two actor sons, of whom Ryan was the perfect, golden boy. My grandmother wanted him to be an actor and nothing else. Sure enough, at twenty-three years old, he landed a leading role on the soap opera *Peyton Place,* and the life my grandparents envisioned for him fell right into his lap. He never knew anything different. But sometimes perfection and great success carry their own burden. In his parents' eyes, Ryan could do no wrong.

Somehow in that mix, which bred such early and massive success, maybe my father never learned to cope with sadness or disappointment. I turn mine inward, where it becomes self-destruction. I wonder if Ryan's sadness or disappointment turns to anger.

I TRIED TO give my children outlets for their emotions. Above all, I wanted Kevin, Sean, and Emily to be happy in my home. Sean remembers walking into my apartment as a teenager and immediately knowing that he was in a safe place. The smell of the apartment, the tone of my voice. My home, wherever it was, was always a loving safety zone. It was a place in which they could escape whatever stress they encountered in the outside world.

It's hard to be the bad guy with your kids (and when I say "bad guy," I just mean the one who lays down the law, says no, and generally breaks kids' hearts in small ways that prepare them for the bigger heartbreaks that are sure to come). I wasn't a pushover, but I tried to teach my children how to regulate themselves. When they were young, I spent a lot of time talking to them, finding out what was going on in their lives, letting their needs and desires drive our time together. I had fought for time with my children; I maximized every moment we had. We have always talked a lot. That's it, plain and simple.

SEAN'S FIRST JOB was over and done. It was great that he was working on his singing and taking all his lessons, but I believe that, at a certain point, everyone has to support himself. You need to learn the value of money, how to take responsibility for yourself, and how to deal with people in the world. I wasn't sure if, in leaving the job,

Sean was dodging work, or if he was sincerely trying to figure out his next steps. Either way, I didn't plan on cleaning up his mess for him.

Sean sent an apologetic letter to my friend. When I read it, I felt that Sean had listened to me. But if he didn't find himself a job soon, I didn't know what my next step should be. I realized that by providing Sean financial and emotional support, I was making up for the times I had not been there for him. I hoped he wasn't taking advantage of me, that he was working through issues he hadn't been able to deal with when I was unavailable. Only time would tell.

CHAPTER EIGHTEEN

REGRET

THE 2010 WINTER holidays were upon us, and, as holidays sometimes do, they made me think about what might have been. Thanksgiving dinner itself was too small for words. It was just four of us at the house of a friend from AA: Emily, who was spending her Thanksgiving break with me, Sean, my friend, and I. My father was down the street at a friend's. Kevin couldn't get time off work, so he was with his dad in New York.

Years ago, I had made the decision that I would never force family holidays. I wanted to make it clear to my kids that they had no obligation to be with me on major holidays. This is an all-too-common problem in divorces—the children feel like they should be in two places at once. So I left it up to them to decide how they wanted to spend holidays. If Kevin felt like staying with his father for

Thanksgiving, I knew that he'd be able to balance it out and do what was right for him.

That Thanksgiving, I felt grateful to be with my family. A family. That was my goal, before I was even old enough to think about such things in clear terms. As a child, all I really knew was that I wanted to be rescued. I wanted my life, as it was, to shift. I didn't want to be teased in school for wearing dirty clothes or tell tall tales about myself in a misguided effort to fit in. I wanted to be nurtured and loved.

Lo and behold, I found early and unheard-of success as a child actor. The attention and accolades presented an amazing opportunity, and maybe if I'd been loved and supported, I could have taken all that opportunity and thrived. But it wasn't what I was after. It wasn't what I needed most. I just wanted the close, stable family I'd never had.

Over the summer, Sean and I had gone out to dinner with my father's onetime girlfriend, Anjelica Huston. Anjelica told a story from when I was a kid. I had come to her crying. I said, "My mother called and said she's going to drive the Corvette off the Santa Monica pier." For hours, the household was up in arms, making calls, trying to figure out where Joanna was. Anjelica remembered staring worriedly out the window at the ocean, her mind filling with gruesome images of my mother's body floating to shore. At some point, I walked over to stand next to her.

She pulled me close and said, "Are you okay? Are you okay?"

Apparently, the shock of the initial phone call had worn off. I was perfectly calm. I said, "Of course I'm okay. Don't worry. Trust me. My mom's not going to do it. She just wants to upset everyone."

At dinner, Anjelica, reflecting on the moment, said, "You were like a cunning adult." I was twelve.

As I look back on those days, I forget how much I could take. I forget how many hugely traumatic things were happening to me on a daily basis and how resilient I was. Today, it astounds me. But that resilience belied what was lying underneath. I was always in a state of semi-shock. Getting that kind of phone call from my mother was run-of-the-mill.

Only during my twenties, in therapy, did I begin to realize that I'd held on to those feelings. I lived in pain until I met cocaine, which briefly brought relief, and it was a completely new and deceptively wonderful sensation for me. The rest of the time I spent in a constant state of apprehension, waiting for the other shoe to drop. I lived in fear that someone was going to yell, accuse, hurt, crash, or die.

And then I met John. I ran into John's arms because I loved him, and in his world I found an oasis of calm and a reason to be on the planet. He was my protector. I cut off contact with my family. It is easy to remember a failed marriage as an unmitigated disaster, but I also realize that it was the most stable time of my life. We had the kids. We had a structure. We created a family. John loved me. He couldn't abide my father, and when he kept me away from him—or tried to—I knew that he did so out of anger for the past and a desire to protect me. I have no doubt he loved me in all the best ways his heart allowed.

Despite the love we had for each other, it soon became clear that John was threatened by my spirit and opinions. I was only nineteen when we met, but as the marriage progressed, I started to come into myself. As I approached thirty, I was finally in great physical shape. I felt popular and confident. John didn't like that I went to social events by myself when he was busy. My self-assurance seemed to threaten him. Some of the mothers at Trinity, the kids' school, said,

"Who cares what he's doing to you? You've got five houses and anything you want." But I cared about more than money. Eventually, I wanted out of my marriage. It just wasn't working.

I wish that I hadn't left John in such an abrupt way. After having been married for nine years, I was done. I refused to work on the marriage. Had I not endured so much with my parents, I believe we could have worked through our problems, or at least given the marriage the effort it deserved. But by the time John got me, I'd been pushed so far that my threshold was close at hand. Anything that made me feel attacked, assaulted, or vulnerable made me flee. I didn't have the resilience that marriage requires of both partners.

When it came to the divorce and custody battle, I didn't anticipate John's training as a competitor. I was blindsided by the ugliness that ensued. Oh, John McEnroe is a formidable opponent. He absolutely refused to lose. That custody battle took everything out of me.

Leaving John meant spending time apart from my children, something I had never imagined from the day Kevin was born. One time it was my weekend to have the children, and John was away on a trip. John had married the singer Patty Smyth. I said something that Patty didn't like, and she kept the kids for the weekend. It was a Friday night at seven P.M. There was no way to get a judge or lawyer at that time of day.

When the children and I were apart, in that unexpected emptiness, all the trauma I'd suppressed exploded like a volcano. I was in total despair, and I was utterly vulnerable to a numbing chemical like heroin, which quieted the sadness, hysteria, and all the feelings that had been hiding under the surface all that time.

I was very alone during those years in New York. If my ex-husband had called me and said he wanted to sit down and talk to me about my substance abuse, I would have listened. He knew I had nobody, but he couldn't or wouldn't do it. He just wasn't that kind of guy. My addiction was not John's fault, but our legal battles definitely didn't help.

There came a time when I ran out of fight. I hadn't been with my children in seven months. I moved from hotel to hotel, to the Venice house where they sued me for installing too many locks, then to a bungalow in West Hollywood. In that bungalow, I wrote a note to John. I was angry at him for ruining my life. Blame, blame, blame. I scrawled the note in a fury, then took an enormous shot of coke. I remember falling down, hitting my head on the floor, and seeing my life flash before me: the past I couldn't change, the choices I regretted, the years I'd missed with my kids. I realized that this wasn't what I wanted to do with what was left of my life. When I came to, I ripped up the letter I'd written to John. To blame him for my life seemed to strip me of the option to change it. I didn't want to give him that power. I called a friend and he came with me to a treatment center to start the process of getting well.

My New York sponsor, Sandy, saw the tug-of-war between me and my ex-husband and said, "Let go of the rope with John. He will fall down and you will be in a place to have the time and space to work on yourself and your addictions." She was right—tug-of-war is horrendous. (Especially if you're playing it with a world champion sportsman who can't lose.) I needed to fight the battle within myself, with me and my demons, my addiction, my self-hate—not with him. From then on, I stopped fighting. I said, *Test me. Put someone in a room with me when I pee. I will do whatever it takes.* I let my kids know that I was in a battle for my life, and that it wasn't about them or their father. I let my kids be angry at the fact that I had problems, but I didn't let them see my problems as permission to treat me badly.

It's obvious to me now that my addiction was not John's fault. But I think it's fair to say there was a battle, and I simply was not up to the challenge. Ultimately, the only good answer for me was to get sober. Sobriety and time brought an end to the saga of drug testing and acrimony.

John won many of our legal skirmishes. But on that Thanksgiving in L.A., looking at my son and daughter, I felt like, in the long run, I had won the war. I had won back my life and my sense of self. For all my regrets, I had what I wanted: relationships with my three children, collectively and separately. I had their respect and love. They genuinely wanted to spend Thanksgiving with me. They chose to do it out of love, not guilt. And that is the best reason of all.

THE DAY AFTER Thanksgiving, Emily, Sean, and I went to Urth Café in West Hollywood for lunch. Emily was wearing a black coat with a brown faux fur collar, which had belonged to Farrah and that my father had given to me. She looked beautiful. Out of the blue, she said, "Mom, I guess you don't remember my final Choreo-lab. It's really too bad, because it was my best one." I knew what she was talking about. Choreo-lab was a modern choreography and dance class that Emily had taken in high school. Every year they had a recital, during which each dancer had a brief solo performance. I went every year. While I attended her final show in 2009, I was on Ativan, an antianxiety pill that had been prescribed to me prior to my neck surgery so that I wouldn't clench my shoulders and tighten my vertebrae. It had been prescribed, but it had been problematic.

Then came the hardest part. Emily told me that when she went onstage, she had tears in her eyes. She could tell that I wasn't myself. When she said that to me, tears sprang to my own eyes. It broke my heart to think that she walked on the stage at her school for her dance recital knowing that I wasn't well and feeling unhappy because of me. Oh, why couldn't I go back in time? Why couldn't I have been the woman I am today with these kids? Every moment of their lives was important. How could I grieve this loss, endure it, and trust that she wasn't broken forever in the way that I had been broken by my parents' behavior?

Emily had been up there alone. She had needed me. I hadn't been there.

Sean, who saw how Emily's story about Choreo-lab had affected me, said, "Oh, Emily, Mom's trying."

But I said, "It's okay, Sean. I want Emily to be able to tell me what she was going through her senior year." I didn't defend my behavior or make excuses. I agreed with Emily. It was sad. At the same time that it pained me to no end to hear what Emily had to say, I saw that it was an important step for us. What a triumph for her to tell me how she felt, to revisit the loneliness of that moment and, with hope, to let it go. She believed in my sobriety. Mom's addiction was done. It had run its course. That confidence allowed Emily, like Sean, to be vulnerable in her own way. She knew she could share and vent, and I would take it as my own and we would move forward. I didn't want her walking around with resentments. I was strong and capable enough of hearing whatever she had to say.

Emily said, "I've forgiven you. I'm so glad I have you now."

Through the nineties, when I was in and out of sobriety, at times I thought, *Someday, Tatum, you're going to regret this situation right here.* I'm there now, full of regret, wishing I could have that time back with my daughter and my sons. Sean, at twenty-three, lives down the street from me and often comes over for dinner. We both feel a need to compensate for the time we missed. As the oldest child, Kevin bore the brunt of my and his father's divorce. My guilt about that will never go away. Kevin knows my regrets and I know his.

I can't change what's done. I can't go back and reclaim the time we lost. All I can do is take solace in knowing that I didn't lose my children forever. They understand that I never stopped fighting to get clean and sober, for myself and for them. After we finished our lunch at Urth, Emily went back to my apartment to do some schoolwork. Sean and I headed to Target to find him a space heater. I admire, respect, and adore these humans and try to be there on every level for them. I grieve over the lost moments, hours, days. I cry for them. One day I will get to the point where I forgive myself for being a junkie, but I'm not there yet.

CHAPTER NINETEEN

AN UNREPENTANT GHOST

AFTER EMILY WENT back to college, I decided to go to the beach house to see Ryan. I needed to keep trying to get close to him. Our show went on a long break for the holidays, so I hadn't seen him for a couple of weeks and I wanted to check on him and to keep the relationship going.

I was in my gym clothes when I arrived, so I decided to work out for a few minutes on my father's exercise bike. Then my father poked his head in the door and said that a man I'll call "Gavin" was coming over. *Gavin.*

Gavin is the same guy who, on a singularly devastating night, gave me drugs and molested me. I was twelve. Gavin was one of my father's oldest friends, and Gavin lived just down the street, and Gavin was on his way. *Good timing, Tatum.*

I didn't waste time blaming my father for inviting Gavin over when I was there. I was too busy scrambling to prepare myself. If Gavin was already on his way, that gave me five minutes to decide what to do. Should I hop in my car and flee, or should I finish my workout? I felt a rush of certainty that I needed to get out of the house. But, for reasons I was too flustered to understand at the time, I stayed.

Anyone who has been molested has his or her own experience of it. The memories of when I was violated make me feel dirty. I feel like I had something to do with it. I thought it was my fault. I'm still battling that sense of all-encompassing culpability.

I was still upstairs on the bike when I heard the front door open and shut with a solid thud. Gavin was in the house. He had hurt me.

It's important to admit that, as I came down the stairs to face Gavin in the kitchen, I thought about the prescription pills for my father's injured back that I knew were in the bathroom closet. Molestation and addiction are frequent partners in crime, because one is an unbearably painful experience and the other promises to liberate you from it. When faced with the past, using is an obvious choice, a quick fix for the discomfort of the moment. Leave your body instead of reliving the damage done to it.

My addiction has the best intentions. It wants to protect me from feelings I can't deal with. Instead, I can be subdued. But addiction is just another molester in disguise.

I was about to come face-to-face with my assailant. Despite all the time I've spent in therapy, I haven't yet done all the work I need to truly accept my innocence in the matter. Since, to my mind, it's still my fault, the memory makes me want to obliterate myself. All the good work I've done to be the woman I want to be went out the window as I walked down those stairs because I blame myself for what happened to me when I was twelve.

I was in an environment that felt unsafe, but don't get me wrong. As I thought about the pills in that closet, I wasn't remotely close to using. Subduing those thoughts with drugs or alcohol is no longer an option for me.

A sober mind makes sober decisions. As I prepared to face Gavin, a little prayer came to me: *God, please relieve me of this moment and help me to survive. I'm with someone who abused me as a twelve-year-old. Help me get to the other side.* I knew I would get there. I put on a happy face and knew I could get through the moment.

When I reached the kitchen, Gavin looked up and nodded at me as if this were an everyday encounter. He and my father continued their conversation about whether it would be fun for Gavin to appear on our show. Oh yeah, that would be a blast. My stomach lurched and bile rose to my throat. I made a mental note to make sure that never happened. Still, inexplicably, I stayed where I was, an unchained prisoner.

When my father left the room to let the dog out, Gavin turned to me. Was he going to address our past? I hoped not. Instead, he said, "How are you, Tatum?"

"Fine, thanks," I said, and that was all. I let surface words and emotions pass for a few minutes until I could make my exit. I chose to forgive him in my heart, but that didn't mean I wanted to be near him for a moment longer.

When I called Patty that night, I told her that I didn't know why I had stayed at the house. Patty said, "Give yourself a break. You don't have to be so hard on yourself. It's okay if you don't always make the right decision."

When I am forced to face painful memories of my past, it helps to accept that whatever my journey is, it's not up to me. I remind myself that each of us has our own god, our own higher power, our own path. I believe that I have a god, ever-mindful and ever-guiding. And that's how I live with it.

Afterward, I stayed safe in my circle of friends, putting one foot in front of the other. I dealt with life on life's terms. I got through it and found that, once again, I was okay. I used to be so terrified to feel negative emotions that I would use before I let myself experience and process real sensations of desperation, sadness, and loss. They are not pleasant feelings, but in choosing to live through them, I am choosing to live. In forgiving even my worst victimizers, I was deciding not just to survive but to move forward.

CHAPTER TWENTY

DISCONNECT

I TRY TO make the best out of every situation, and I was looking for friends who did the same. I had assorted friends through my meetings and otherwise, but I didn't have the fully formed group of female friends that I wanted. Friendships have never come easily to me, especially friendships with women. When I'm in my bluest of blues, I think, *God, I have been alone my entire life.* My relationship with my mother instilled in me a sense of longing for connection followed immediately by mistrust. That pattern was replicated throughout my youth and is still at play today.

Kids pick up skills on the playground as they make their first friendships, and sort and re-sort themselves over the school years. I missed out on those valuable lessons, as I never really had the opportunity to be a child, much less a child who played with other children.

In 1972, when I arrived at boarding school after leaving my mother's ranch, it was the first time I'd really been exposed to other kids (unless you count the teenage delinquents my mother harbored, which I don't). I was an uncivilized little scalawag without any sense of how children were expected to look or act. My shoes, if I remembered to put them on, were invariably on the wrong feet. My hair stuck out in all directions. I had a weird, robotic affect when I spoke.

After *Paper Moon* was filmed, I went to a new school, the Ojai Valley School. I was a friendless urchin-freak there, just as I had been at Tree Haven. But when the movie hit theaters nationwide, my stardom suddenly outshone my social awkwardness and I found some friends. I was relieved to be accepted, but I wasn't an idiot. I knew they liked me only for my newfound fame. It was a sudden, obvious shift. I got that what they liked was my celebrity, not necessarily me.

My life with my father—starring in *Paper Moon* and all that followed—transformed me, but instead of becoming an everyday schoolgirl, I became a quiet, watchful girl-woman who, rather than make age-appropriate friends with my peers, set my sights on connecting with my father's girlfriends and other women in our shared world.

Once, when Ryan took me on a trip to Acapulco, I stole anything I could grab out of our hostess's bathroom. I was ten and years away from dropping the nasty stealing habit I'd picked up at boarding school. Ryan came up to me and said, "Tatum, where's all the stuff?"

I said, "The stuff? I didn't steal anything!" The truth was written all over my face. I was a ten-year-old, not a criminal.

Ryan said, "If you don't tell me . . ."

"Okay, okay," I said. "It's under the bed."

I had no idea at the time why I did it—what does a preteen want with perfume or makeup?—but now it's clear to me. I didn't want friends my own age. I wanted a mother, a female role model. I wanted Cher, Bianca Jagger, Ursula Andress, Anouk Aimée. I tried to pull these women closer. Stealing was a way to appropriate their stuff and habits. Looking back, it's a pretty funny assembly of female role models, but I tried on their shoes, I borrowed their clothes, I stole their perfume, I thought of them as friends. I was an unrepentant thief until I was fourteen, when I was shooting *International Velvet* in London and I almost got busted in an Yves Saint Laurent shop taking a shirt. I look back and laugh at myself now—I haven't stolen anything in thirty-three years.

My father and Anjelica Huston started dating when I was twelve. They were together for several years. She used to take me horseback riding when I was getting ready for the movie *International Velvet*. I loved and adored her, and, as always, was fixated on the elements of her femininity.

When Sean and I had gone to dinner with Anjelica over the summer, as I kissed her hello I asked, "Do you still wear Miss Dior?" Though we've seen each other many, many times over the years, I'm sure she was thinking, *Oh my God, Tatum is still obsessed with my perfume after all this time.*

WHEN I WAS a teenager, I discovered that some people, mostly women, befriended me to get to Ryan. That was an eye-opener, and I discovered that there was a safety in people who were already known or successful on their own terms. When I dated Andy Gibb and Michael Jackson, I knew they weren't going out with me because of who I was. They didn't need me. The same was true with John. He wasn't attracted by my fame. If anything, he wanted it to go away. He was too famous as it was.

When John and I got married, we traveled constantly to tennis tournaments around the world. I'd grown up surrounded by men, and on the tennis circuit, it was more of the same. I spent most of the time with John and his brothers, and then my first two babies were boys. It was fun being a guy's girl.

I didn't have much of a chance to establish real bonds with people in New York. Even if I'd had the opportunity to make friends, I'm not sure I really knew how. But at the time I didn't notice or mind the isolation—John and I were busy with his international career and our growing family.

With the divorce, whatever connections I'd formed in New York were pretty much severed. Those relationships, it turned out, were the kind that money or fame often attract. We were surrounded by people whose livelihoods benefited from friendship with us. These friendships can certainly be and often are genuine—a realtor, a home designer, an art dealer—but when it came to the divorce, those mutual friends and acquaintances unanimously sided with John.

Eventually, I did make a few real friends in New York—most notably, Kyle. When I go to New York, I always stay with Kyle. I love Kyle's energy. He is funny and ambitious and always upbeat. When we are together, we sing and dance and go to movies and the theater. And watch reality television. Above all, Kyle is loyal and dedicated in a way that's indescribable. In my whirlwind life I have met all sorts of people in all different walks of life, but in Kyle I found a soul mate. But now, Kyle was leading a very busy life in New York and I was in L.A.

Spending my childhood in the company of adults and being somewhat isolated in my marriage left me with a hollow feeling. When I published *A Paper Life,* I set free the garbage barge of damage that I had dragged behind me for so many years. Afterward, I felt lucky to have survived. I walked with a lighter step and a softer heart. I wasn't so watchful and protective, worried about what might happen next. I was finding that it worked better in the world to bring a smile to the table. It sounds cheesy, coming from a woman with tattoos and hardcore drugs in her past. But I was really trying to change. I wanted to make new choices, to find a better life. That meant trying to explore opportunities I'd missed, like having strong female friendships.

I had grown up in L.A., and I thought I was returning to a place where I had old, loyal friends. But years had passed. I had struggled and grown, and maybe the simple truth of the matter is that, during my years in New York, I had grown away from my old friends.

As I spent time with old and new friends, it was hard to know whom to trust. Did people like me, Tatum, or did they like "Tatum O'Neal"? I knew to watch out for people who were interested in me for fame's sake. This became all too apparent when I started working on the docudrama. Some friends were overexcited, to say the least. Nobody blatantly came up to me and said, "Hey, I want to be on TV! Can I be on TV with you? Huh? Can I?" Actually, I wouldn't have minded that. Especially if it might help their careers. I respect ambition. Instead, they insinuated themselves into my life, not-so-subtly reminding me how very close we'd *always* been.

. . . .

IN AA THERE were other complications that arose among my friendships. One of the hardest was when I noticed that I hadn't been hearing from my friend Tony. I was concerned. Tony struggled with his sobriety, but he'd been doing really well. He was very involved in AA, and he was feeling good about it. He had been sober for almost ninety days. But I had lent him some money, and when I didn't hear from him, I worried that he was spending the loan on drugs.

I started calling and texting him, telling him how worried I was and asking him to just let me know that he was all right.

When I didn't hear back, I finally called his boyfriend. He said, "Tony's fine. He's just sleeping." But somehow I knew he was lying.

I said, "Put him on the phone," but his boyfriend refused.

THE NEXT DAY, I continued my campaign, texting our mutual friends to find out if they'd heard from Tony. Nobody had heard a single word. Finally, Tony shot me a short text: "I'm fine. Leave me alone. Stop bugging me Tatum." Then I knew for certain something was wrong.

I texted Tony, saying, "Here's the thing, Tony. If you didn't use, which is what you're saying, then where are you? Usually we speak at least once a day. What's going on? Why did you just disappear? Something must have happened. As a friend, I'm curious." No response.

I was devastated. Knowing that he was in danger and not hearing back from him was scary. Not only was I worried about Tony, but I also wondered about the friendship. It was hard enough for me to make friends. Why did I pick people who were unavailable? When I called Patty to talk about it, she wondered if God put Tony in my life to show me what it feels like when your loved ones use. Maybe it was a lesson for me: *See this? This is something you never want to make your children endure again.*

Finally, Tony e-mailed to say, "I didn't tell you the truth—I did get high." After this confession, Tony, caught up in the chaos and drama of his relapse, started texting me like crazy, asking what people were saying about him at meetings. I didn't want to gossip with him. I just said, "Whatever you're doing to stay sober isn't working. Is it your self-esteem? Your boyfriend? Your therapist? I don't know what you're planning to do differently, but something big has to change." Unless he had an epiphany, he wouldn't be able to stay sober for any length of time.

My emotions surrounding Tony's relapse were split. While having a friend in jeopardy upset me, of course, the opportunity to support him made me feel proud and capable. That feeling inspired me to keep fighting in order to be strong for him—and any other friends who decided to come back to sobriety and wanted help doing so. If they wanted to jump on my lifeboat, I was right there, but I was not going down with them.

When I told Patty what was going on, she suggested that I take a thirty-day break from Tony until he got himself better. I needed to have clearly defined relationships. I didn't want to be sucked into the world of relapse, which is full of lies and deceit. But Patty's recommendation wasn't just for the sake of protecting me. It was important to show Tony that if he couldn't stay sober, he couldn't be part of my life. Tony was a successful businessman and a compelling guy. It was easy for him to convince me and everyone else around him that he was dedicated to his sobriety, but, as we all knew, he'd been relapsing every three to six months for the last five years. In a 12-step program, where there are people who have been sober for twenty to thirty years, there isn't much tolerance for people who continually take from the program without ever giving back to it. Someone who relapses chronically starts to feel like a burden. Maybe it would help Tony to see that if he continued to do this, he would eventually exhaust our support. He would lose all his friends. Tough love actually works sometimes. Much as we wanted to help him, at some point he had to commit. If he stayed with the program, he would have the love and safety of a group that was doing exactly what he was doing. Much as I wanted to be there for my friend, I listened to Patty, kept my distance, and prayed for Tony.

Boundaries aren't hard for me with friends—intimacy is. Even when it came to people I trusted, I wasn't used to having them in my life. I didn't have the ordinary habits of friendship that most people have. Much as I love Patty, I even struggle with calling and engaging with her as much as I could. I have trouble answering the simplest questions. If she asks how I am (and Patty isn't just being polite—she really means it when she asks), I'm not sure of the answer. It's difficult for me to know exactly how I feel. How am I? Am I good? I think I'm good. In the past, when I didn't feel good, my father insisted that I was fine. Maybe I should have been fine. But I know that life and friendships can grow and thrive in spite of such self-doubt and hesitation. I feel grateful to have Patty in my life and to know that I can turn to her, and most of the time, I do.

I wanted to connect with people who challenged themselves and always tried to move forward. I'd found wonderful support from friends at my meetings, but I still imagined myself surrounded by a pack of strong, awesome women, preferably women who had had children, women who wanted to work, women who were ambitious and funny, women who didn't feel sorry for themselves. I finally felt ready, and it was getting easier to connect, but I was busy with the show, and it was hard to make time. I had Emily, Patty, and a few other trusted and fun confidantes. For now, that was enough.

CHAPTER TWENTY-ONE

THE NEW GENERATION

WITH HIS FIRST job behind him, Sean turned all his energy back to his true goal: acting. When Sean was in high school, I took him to plays like *Doubt, Pillow Man,* and *Glengarry Glen Ross.* Seeing those plays, Sean connected to the actors. He started reading about Montgomery Clift, Marlon Brando, Paul Newman, Henry Fonda, William Holden, and James Dean, as well as the director Elia Kazan; he watched every one of their films more than once. These were his heroes, and he wanted to follow in their footsteps. Sean had been bitten by the acting bug.

Sean's dedication is really quite extraordinary—more focused and serious than mine ever was. For me, acting was a way to escape school. Beyond that, I had no idea what I was getting myself into. I didn't know that every director wouldn't be like Peter Bogdanovich, saying, "Hey, Tatesky, when you look at that guy, look at him like *this*." I came to grips with that on my second movie, *Bad News Bears*, when the director didn't act out the scenes for me. As I matured, it dawned on me that acting was a vocation, not just a get-out-of-school-free card. Could I do it? Did I want to? Eventually, I went to New York to figure out if I wanted to be an actor as an adult. But Sean made an informed decision after completing high school and college. He chose acting as a young man. He would have a very different experience, and I looked forward to that for him.

Being a twenty-three-year-old would-be actor in Los Angeles is not the most straightforward career choice in the world. So, at the same time as I tried to support Sean's efforts, I urged him to get a job in order to support himself. I tried to let him know that the day might come when I would stop helping him pay the bills.

I heard about all the details of Sean's efforts to break into the industry, but so far no work had materialized. I myself had never broken into the industry the hard way, so all I could do was place my hope alongside Sean's and try to come up with ideas where I could.

One day I came home after a day of writing, working on the show, and going to the gym. I was in desperate need of a nap. Just as I was drifting off, I heard Sean's key in the door. He sat down on my bed and said, "Mom, I had a fender bender." I sat up. He looked fine and quickly reassured me that nobody was hurt.

The woman had taken a picture of the license plate with her cell phone. The car was registered to me. I envisioned the cops coming to the door at any moment. As I sat there trying to wrap my head around that, Sean's phone rang. It was his manager. He had an audition for *Law & Order*.

This was good news, but Sean was dumbfounded by the combination of good and bad events. When he hung up the phone, his face turned bright red. He was heading for what he calls a Level Ten Tantrum. It's not easy to be John McEnroe's son and Ryan O'Neal's grandson. Sean inherited some of his father's perfectionist tendencies and his inability to lose at anything. He has a tendency to blow up before thinking a situation through. And then there's what Sean gets from me. I am no shrinking violet, and I have a temper. So Sean, from the get-go, had TNT in his DNA. If undirected and undisciplined, that can lead to total disaster. But, in our family at least, success has gone hand in hand with force of personality. If channeled correctly, it can lead to total greatness.

The first part I ever auditioned for was in *Urban Cowboy*. I was auditioning for the part Debra Winger would play, and at fifteen I was young for it. At the time, I was living in a house on Beverly Grove, up above Beverly Hills, with Ryan and Griffin. I wasn't going to high school. I had asked my father if I could drop out, because everyone else was doing drugs. He said, "Okay." Instead, I stayed home, reading the books that my father and Peter Bogdanovich gave me: *Great Expectations, Wuthering Heights, The Catcher in the Rye, From Here to Eternity.*

Sue Mengers had been my agent ever since *Paper Moon,* but she had married Jean-Claude Tramont and was moving to Paris, so nobody was paying much attention to my career. The night before the audition, somebody (probably my father) said, "Tatum, tomorrow you're going to an audition." A messenger delivered the pages from the script, but I had no idea what to do with them, so they just sat in their envelope in the front hall, like any old piece of mail. The next morning, I put on high heels that I'd gotten at Theodore's and a cotton skirt. John Travolta had just done *Saturday Night Fever*. Because I knew Travolta was going to be in the movie, and I wanted to get the part, I abstained from smoking pot that morning. At the time, I thought that counted as an effort at professionalism. I drove myself to the audition, tried to do what they asked of me, and drove myself back home. Needless to say, I didn't get the part.

As Sean's stage mother I tried not to get overly involved, but I wanted to be there for him. I might give him a hint here or there, but I didn't usually give him line readings. I trusted his instincts as they were and his ability to develop them further. Really, if I thought he'd be disappointed in what acting had to offer, that it might not make him happy, or that he wasn't cut out for it, I would tell him. For better or worse, I'm relentlessly honest. Kevin thinks a white lie is appropriate if you don't like someone's haircut, but I can't do it. I don't know how else to be.

I ran lines with him, made us dinner, and then ran lines with him some more until he knew his part by heart. The next morning, I sent him a text saying, "You did great last night. I'm really proud of you." Later I sent another: "Good luck today. Let me know how it goes." I meant what I said sincerely, and at the same time I was aware that these were simple phrases, the obvious words of support that a parent feeds a child. It crossed my mind that I would have loved to hear words like that growing up. I would have loved to have someone I could go to with my fears. Someone who would support me and give me encouragement.

Sean would pay for the fender bender with money he had saved from his modeling days, but, sadly, he wouldn't get the *Law & Order* part. Regardless, it felt good to correct the course with my son. Sean's self-esteem and confidence were intact. That would serve him well as an actor. I was glad he wouldn't go into his auditions with the doubt I knew so well.

That night, when he finally felt good about the lines he'd practiced, Sean went home; I walked Pickle and went to sleep. Although he went home to his own apartment, it was like Sean and I were back in another phase of life, with me taking care of him, helping him with his homework, and seeing him through the mistakes a kid makes as he's figuring it all out. I minded, because my own life was tiring enough, and yet I didn't mind one little bit.

CHAPTER TWENTY-TWO

RYAN'S EYES

WITH DECEMBER CAME a rare rainy winter, casting an unfamiliar shadow across Los Angeles. The show was still on a holiday break, and it was a good thing, because I wasn't feeling well. After a week of what I thought was the flu, I took a turn for the worse and was diagnosed with strep and pneumonia.

Then my father called and invited me to the beach house. I didn't want to be sick and alone in my apartment for Christmas. Who needs that? So I took Pickle and Wallis and went to the beach house to convalesce—still, in some way, that little girl who wanted a parent to take care of her when she was sick. My father was happy to see me and—to my amazement—was a dedicated and enthusiastic nurse. He got food from the market and brought it up to me on a tray. He rubbed my neck to relieve my nausea. He managed the remote control but ceded movie selection to me.

When I wasn't hungry for dinner, Ryan came in with a steaming bowl and said, "You need two bites of turkey soup." He spoon-fed me, just because he wanted me to have something in my stomach. I really wasn't hungry, but I let him feed me anyway. I had endured so many years of wanting to be taken care of, of longing to be nurtured by my father, that this was a dream come true. After all that, it was the best soup I'd ever tasted.

Most of all, Ryan made me laugh. As always, he talked to my cat, Wallis, as if she understood the entire English language. He'd say, "Wally, come and eat. No, don't go that way, come this way. No, Wally, the food isn't in the bathroom. Come and get on my lap. Good, Wally, good." And, like a little kid, he was clearly dying to tell me what he'd gotten me for Christmas but trying as hard as he could not to spill the beans.

Although I could tell Ryan liked having my company at the beach house, he hadn't changed overnight. One time my father was out getting lunch for us when I texted him, asking where something was. He wrote back, ALL CAPS, "I'M ON MY WAY BACK SO WHAT DO YOU WANT TATUM?"

He sounded so angry. As a joke, I wrote, "Are you coming to kill me?" But when he came home, he said he was trying to type as fast as he could at a red light. At least we were making light of our problems—wasn't that a good sign?

IN SOME WAYS my father's house is a shrine to the best of times we had together. On every wall, there are pictures of us and the rest of the family in our golden days. The original poster from *Paper Moon*,

Andy Warhol's portrait of Farrah. My father making a funny face at me, a toddler, as he does chin-ups in a park somewhere. Ryan and me going to a party, his shirt unbuttoned to show off his chest. In the seventies, my father took me everywhere with him.

As we got ready to fly to Kansas and be costars on *Paper Moon,* my father had his first taste of being a full-time single father. I was eight years old. Now that I had him, I wasn't going to let him out of my sight. I insisted on going everywhere he went.

"Where're you going?" I'd ask.

"I'll be back. I've hired a babysitter," he'd say.

"No, I have to go with you. Or I'll run away. Come on, I have to go with you." And so, not knowing anything else, he brought me along. I went to parties, to premieres, to concerts. I saw Rod Stewart and the Faces and fell in love with the guitarist Ron Wood. I got to see the Who and meet Mick Jagger.

No doubt I cramped Ryan's style. On the beach one day, we ran into Nancy Reagan, who was at the time the first lady of California. As he was chatting politely with her, I kept saying, "Let's go, let's go! I want to play ball." On Sunday nights, we went to the Playboy Mansion to watch the new movie releases. Ryan says I made absolutely sure that there were no Bunnies in his life.

Before we started making *Paper Moon,* we went to a Christmas party at Alana Stewart's house. (We had no idea at the time that Alana would one day be Farrah Fawcett's best friend and a close friend of Ryan's.) There was a Nicaraguan actress at the party who took an interest in Ryan. He thought she was stunningly beautiful. Ryan says I watched their interaction, then insisted that he take me home alone. Immediately. He asked why I wouldn't let him have a girlfriend. I said, "I can't help it, Dad."

He said, "You want me to be alone?"

I said, "You're not alone. You're with me."

ONE AFTERNOON, AS we took a walk on the beach, Ryan himself was the one to bring up the one time we ever tried to go to therapy together. Therapy was the topic that had last thrown us off-balance, but now we approached it calmly. I went to a psychiatrist, Dr. Foster, for the first time in my teen years. At her request I brought my father to a session, but it ended with him declaring himself my savior and walking out in the middle of the hour. Ryan asked if that therapy had been helpful to me. He knew that Dr. Foster had told me to get away from him. I said yes.

Thinking about therapy, and what it does for people, I asked Ryan why he had so much anger. I wondered if there was something about his childhood, or the way he saw the world, that I didn't know. Ryan didn't answer my question directly, but he said, "I'm not just angry at you. I'm angry at everybody. I'm a fighter. I fight with every-body." I tried to imagine what it was like going through life with that feeling. He was a boxer in body and spirit. He was so different from my ex-husband, who restrained himself as long as he could until he exploded. Ryan just let out smoke as he barreled forward.

It was midday, but the December sun was pale and forgiving. We seemed to be in a safe zone, probing tender issues without exploding, so I brought up my teenage years.

When you get to my age, the best and worst moments of your life become a little like a greatest hits album. You've heard them too many times. You don't want them to define you. You long to play something, anything else. But still, in a way, they shape who you are and how you are perceived. With Ryan, I kept circling that period of my life, hoping to get some kind of acknowledgment. I felt like he had to recognize how painful that time had been for me if I were to ever move past it into forgiveness.

For now, I asked Ryan why he had left me alone at sixteen.

His explanation was, "That's what you wanted, sweetie. You were begging me to have your own place. I was just doing what you told me to do."

I said, "Dad, I was sixteen."

He said, "You were the most mature sixteen-year-old I'd ever met. You'd been to Paris, to London. You were an Academy Award winner. You knew what to do."

He still believed that a sixteen-year-old was perfectly capable of parenting herself, or that was his best argument and he was sticking to it. Then he said, "God, I just loved Farrah so much." He declared his love for her frequently, often spontaneously, but in this moment it was part of his explanation. Ryan went on to say that when he met Farrah, I made him choose between us. "How do you choose to be away from Farrah? I thought I'd died and gone to heaven. You and I had been side by side for six years. I was hungry like a wolf for a love story."

He stopped walking and turned to look at me with sad eyes. "It was a terrible time in my life, to be pulled in both directions like that. After all those years of taking care of you by myself, I felt like it was my turn."

I disagreed. Just because a sixteen-year-old says "choose" doesn't mean a parent has to accept that choice. It was hurtful to hear that his love for Farrah was what motivated him. It was like he was saying, *I'm sorry I deserted you, but I was busy playing with Barbie.*

But in his mind it had come from me. I had forced the choice on him. Hard as it was, I tried to accept that as his true experience.

Then he added, "You were sixteen, then seventeen, and you were going through all kinds of changes that I wasn't comfortable with. I didn't quite understand all this growth-hormone stuff. The boyfriends. Michael Jackson adored you. That was all right with me. But nobody else."

This was my father, not the all-powerful god I worshipped as a child but a young man saddled with an adolescent daughter he didn't understand. In his own way, he was admitting that he was simply overwhelmed, and he had bowed out. If he had to choose between parenting a tough teenager and enjoying happiness with Farrah, and he thought he did, then the choice was clear to him.

Looking out at the quiet ocean, Ryan said, "I was infuriated when you complained about me being with Farrah. We were a lopsided family. We were winging it. Just like you do in the movies. None of it was by the book. There were no easy answers. Suddenly, something came up that we couldn't handle. You know how people always ask if you'd do anything differently in your life? The usual answer is no. But I would have liked to do that time over. Maybe I could have gotten it right. I knew at the time that I wasn't at my best."

This was huge. In my entire life, this was the first time Ryan had expressed regret. At last, he was admitting that he had made a choice, and that it affected me. It was the closest he'd ever come to taking responsibility for some of the trauma of my youth. A morsel!

Yet, as he took responsibility, he cast blame. Ryan said, "You were against my relationship with Farrah. You didn't see it as the great love story that I did. To prove it, you left town, and when you came back, you didn't contact any of us. Not even my mother, your grandmother. That hurt me the most. You walked away from people who cared for you to marry someone who didn't love you the way a woman should be loved.

"And your hatred for me grew. With no contact, it just grew. I didn't even get invited to your wedding. I never imagined that. When you had your first baby, I thought you'd see how hard it was and give me a pass on my mistakes, and then we could reunite. Farrah was all for it. She saw how hurt I was and knew it was about my daughter.

"When I made *Paper Moon* with you, I knew that would bond us forever. It was hell, and we came out the other side, heroes. We saw the worst and best of each other, every day, day after day. But I was wrong. You moved on and took no prisoners. I had to erase you from my mind, my heart.

"Where were you for twenty-five years? I try not to think about that. It's too late. But I'm still healthy. Maybe we'll have another twenty-five and make the best of it."

I looked at my father and just said, "I hope so, Dad. Twenty-five years would be nice." We had been walking for a while, and I was pretty sure it wasn't a recommended treatment for pneumonia. I was tired, and we were back at the house, but I went up the stairs with some reluctance. These were conversations that had never happened before. Never. I tried to recognize that as progress even though I didn't like all of what I was hearing. I held my tongue, listened, and kept my emotions in check. He was only human. This was how he felt, and the only way to understand him, us, and myself, was to absorb his point of view, the side that I had never understood. I let his words crowd into my brain, where I would sort them out later. What I heard most clearly was that he loved me, he had missed me, he wanted me in his life, and he was glad to have me back. We shared those feelings. They were a foundation, and I hoped we could build on them.

PART III

GRACE

CHAPTER TWENTY-THREE

EVERYTHING'S PERFECT

MY FATHER HAD expressed regret for one of the pivotal moments of my childhood. The conversation hadn't happened on-camera, but we had made it through tough terrain without disaster, and I had survived it without the security of witnesses. It was the sort of moment I'd hoped for when I began this process.

I wanted a happy ending, and I wish I could end with that. I wish I could end by saying: *I stayed at my father's house. He took me to the doctor. He took care of me. We ate together. We watched movies. We talked.* I wish I could add: *Now my dad and I are doing great. Our whole family spent Christmas together. Everything's perfect. La-di-da.*

This is not that story. This is a story of imperfection and strife. It is a story of struggle and redemption. It is not perfect, but it is real and true.

· · · ·

THE BEACH HOUSE was supposed to be a place for me to recover. All was promising at first. Along the way, that plan went amiss. The more time I spent there, the harder it got. I love the beach, but I stopped enjoying it. I thought it was because I was ill, but the truth was that it was not a good place for me. It was quiet and clean. The peaceful ocean rolled away in the backyard. But behind the big glass windows, we were all in our own worlds. Redmond was in his room. My father was in his room. And I was in my room, caught up in old memories.

THE DAY BEFORE Christmas, I came into the kitchen to talk to Ryan's friend Marketa, who was helping him out with some office work. Ryan was unloading his popsicles and other items into the freezer. As I innocently asked Marketa a question, my father's voice boomed over us, "Hey, what are you doing in here? This is my kitchen time!"

Kitchen time? I had no idea what he was talking about. I said, "Whoa, whoa. I'm just talking to Marketa."

He came right up to me and yelled, "Get out of the kitchen. I'm working, can't you see that?"

"Yes, Dad, I see that," I said. "I'm out of here." I went up to my room.

ABOUT TWENTY MINUTES later, Ryan came into my room and sat down on my bed. He said, "I love you. I don't mean to yell like that." I believed him. My father has man rituals. It turned out that he really didn't like anybody to go into the kitchen during the four minutes it took for him to put away his popsicles. He had a very particular way he liked to store his popsicles in the freezer. Those four minutes were sacred to him. I should have known. But I didn't.

Ryan said, "Tatum, you are too white. I think a spray tan would help."

Ha! I said, "You know, Dad, I don't like the spray tans. I think they look orange and unnatural."

What I really knew was that the problem wasn't on the surface. It was deeper than that. Then Ryan pointed at my leg. He said, "Ooh, is that the scar from the car accident?"

I said, "Yeah."

He said, "It's not that bad." This was far from the truth. The scars I had from the car accident to which he was referring may not have been visible, but they were very deep and lasting.

When I was fifteen, after a night of partying with Mackenzie Phillips, my friend Carrie and I set out to join my father on vacation in Big Sur. Carrie was driving the Jeep that I had leased for my mother. We were on the highway for a while, maybe I had drifted off, maybe I blacked out, but the next thing I knew I was lying on the highway. Carrie had lost control of the car and hit a guardrail. The Jeep tipped, the doors flew open, and the two of us were thrown out into the middle of the road.

The car accident and its aftermath were a dark, dark time for me. All the self-doubt I had inside—about becoming a woman, being worthy, being lovable, having a purpose—rose to the surface.

Soon afterward, Ryan moved in with Farrah, and the line connecting those two events formed a wall between me and my self-esteem, me and my happiness, me and my father, a massive wall of trauma over which I never seemed to be able to climb.

It was not too late to turn this train wreck of a life around, but the car accident had the opposite effect. My self-esteem was forever affected. From the moment of the accident, I saw myself as damaged goods, and I became the despondent daughter of Ryan O'Neal, who walked with her head hung down with the weight of loss and despair. I got stuck in the low until I met cocaine . . . and then John McEnroe.

Now, sitting on the bed, Ryan brought up my scars. I didn't say, *Do you remember that you weren't there for me?* I didn't say that, or anything remotely like it. The way I see it is that if he admitted to being sorry about one thing, he'd have to apologize for everything.

Or this: he didn't see any of it the same way I did. He said he had never read my book, we never talked about it, and for all I knew, he had no idea how hard it had been.

By mentioning the scars, was he tentatively opening a door? Maybe this was it—the opportunity I'd been waiting for. I could articulate my experience. We could begin to merge our different memories of the past. The cameras had been following me and my father. We'd taken some local trips. We'd had plenty of time to talk. But I had been holding back. I let him talk about the past in his rose-tinted way, without reminding him of the dark truths that came up for me at every turn. I was afraid of scaring my father away. But repressing the truth was taking its toll on me. My health was starting to deteriorate. I felt emotionally exhausted. Above all, I was tired of the endless denial. I couldn't listen to his incomplete version of the past any longer.

A few days earlier our talk on the beach had gone well. Now I drew him back to my childhood. During the seventies, starting when I was twelve, our household was chaotic. To some extent, it was a broader problem during that era in Hollywood. Children were left alone. Their parents were out partying, or they were partying around their children and with them. There were no boundaries.

There were many issues to address, but this time I started with Gavin. The one with whom my father blithely still maintained a friendship. "Why didn't you protect me? I was twelve."

He said, "What was I supposed to do, Tatum?"

Only days before he had alluded to his regret, but that sentiment had seemingly passed. Not for the first time, I wanted to write out the words I wanted to hear and hand them to him. A script was what we needed—the script for the third act of the father-daughter play with a happy ending. *Tatum, if I could go back in time and change my behavior, I would. I'd do backbends to create a new life for us so I could have your company and spirit around.*

I wasn't getting anywhere, but I was feeling brave and he, at least, was participating, so I kept trying. I brought us back to how he left me and Griffin to live on our own as teenagers. I'd listened on the beach when he told me that I forced him to choose between me and Farrah. Now it was time for him to hear my side.

I reminded him that during that time he had neglected some basic parenting obligations. "Dad, what school were we going to?"

He said, "You went to Hollywood Professional School."

I said, "Dad, I didn't attend. I never finished school."

He said, "You didn't need school."

I said, "But, Dad, I had Griffin. He was getting into trouble." The police had brought Griffin home repeatedly for car accidents, drugs, and other destructive behavior that showed the toll our lives was taking on him.

He said, "Farrah was intriguing."

Exasperated, I said, "I didn't live with her. She didn't know me. How do you think I felt, Dad? Sensitive? Confused? Abandoned? It was a nightmare." I tried to force him to consider my side. "You say that I made you choose between us, but it's not like you brought us to Farrah's house and showed us our rooms. You never asked us to come live there."

I had been his favorite, his girl, his constant companion. Then I wasn't anymore.

What I was asking for was beyond what he could face. He said, "I was saddled with you children. Sorry, Tate."

A silence fell over the room. As we sat there I looked at his face, still handsome and strong. He worked hard to preserve that movie-star exterior. For all he loved the stories of us as sidekicks—me the scampish kid and him the ladies' man—he had left because we'd outgrown that phase. I was becoming a woman, and he couldn't handle my puberty. As an adolescent, I was a burden to him. That is what I had believed all these years and would believe until I heard different.

Whenever we reached this point, our needle got stuck in its groove, damning us to hear the same warped theme over and over. I wanted Ryan to understand how I had felt as a fifteen-year-old. But that was the heart of the problem. He hadn't known what to do with me when I was fifteen, so what was the point of conversation, now or then?

Having this conversation with my dad got me nowhere. What I was beginning to learn was that I was better off not having it at all.

.　.　.　.

THAT NIGHT I spoke to Patty. In my 12-step program, the first step is admitting that you are powerless over alcohol and your life is unmanageable. Patty always said to me, "You are powerless over Ryan and your life is unmanageable. You can't do anything about his behavior. Stop trying to change it. Stop feeling sorry for yourself about it. Get over it." In the program, we talk about people, places, and things. You stay away from the people, places, and things that lurk at the heart of your addiction. On the exterior, like my father, the beach house looked warm and welcoming, like the right place to go when I was ill, but in it lurked every danger I *knew* I should avoid. Why was I still here?

My father had taken care of me while I was sick, but we hadn't gone to therapy yet. Given our dynamic, I had overstayed my welcome. We simply needed to do some work before we could spend too much time in close quarters. I needed to let go of the past—if I stayed in the present, these small encounters wouldn't feel so loaded. Besides, I was an adult. Sick or well, I belonged in my own home.

MARLEY, A HOUSEKEEPER who has worked for my father for more than twenty years, was down in the kitchen. I went in and made myself a cup of tea. I said to her, "I love my dad, and I love my brother, but I have to go home and face the music, whatever the music is."

I wrote my father a note. *Dad, I love you, and I'll keep trying, but I am too old to be living at home.*

MY FATHER'S HOUSE is beautiful. It is clean and sunny. There are orchids everywhere. Most rooms have a stunning view of the ocean.

In my room, there is a pseudo-weathered sign leaning against the wall. It says: THE BEACH FIXES EVERYTHING. *Ha. I wish!*

I gathered all my stuff, got in the car, and drove back to West Hollywood. It was Christmas Eve and I was back at home, sweet home.

CHAPTER TWENTY-FOUR

MY OWN

ON NEW YEAR'S EVE, Oprah's new network, OWN, threw a launch party. Peter Morgan's boyfriend, Andrew, came over to do my hair. I was wearing a black (there's a shock), long-sleeved dress that showed a little cleavage, a leather jacket, and shoes that my father had given me for Christmas. My hair was curly and parted in the middle. I had on drop gold earrings and an Irish Claddagh ring that I had been looking to for strength. I looked as good as I could on my best day. Andrew and I talked and laughed about what it had been like at the beach house. I felt lucky to have known him and Peter for so long. Andrew and I decided that 2011 had to be a good year for all of us. Enough was enough.

It was a freezing night. I got a call from Redmond saying that he, Ryan, and Ryan's friend Marketa were downstairs, waiting in Ryan's Porsche. I didn't panic, although I know how Ryan hates to wait for anybody. Redmond sounded calm, and I felt confident and good.

I climbed into the backseat next to Marketa. Off we went.

The party was at Soho House, on Sunset Boulevard, not far from my apartment. Ryan told us that he wanted to get there right at dinnertime so he wouldn't have to mingle during cocktails. He pulled up across the street, on Doheny, and stopped the car. He wanted to wait until it was late enough so that we could go straight to dinner.

As we sat in the idling car, Red noticed that Farrah's Saint Christopher medal was hanging on the rearview mirror. He asked to put it on.

Ryan took the necklace off the mirror and handed it to Redmond. I leaned over and fastened it around Red's neck.

At last it was time for my father to make his fashionably late entrance. We drove into the parking garage, gave the car to the valet, and came upon a crowd of people waiting to board the elevators up to Soho House, which is in a gorgeous, glass-walled penthouse. My father said, "Tatum, who are all these people?" I wormed my way through to the front of the line, told them we were on the list, and managed to get Ryan past the line.

Up on the club floor, we entered a private party room where people were having cocktails. I walked in, excited and happy to be there. All the OWN higher-ups were there. It was a great opportunity for me. Lisa, the chief creative officer of OWN, took me by the arm and said, "I want to make sure you're healthy, well, and cared for through this process. The show is secondary to what you're going through." And Rod, the head of programming and development, said, "We believe in you. We love you. Your story is riveting. We're so excited we can't stand it." I glowed in their enthusiasm.

Eventually all the other guests filtered into the room and filled the chairs. The tables had assigned seating. At ours, in addition to the four of us, were Oprah, Steadman, Dr. Phil, and Dr. Phil's wife, Robin McGraw. Soon after everyone was seated, Oprah went to the microphone and gave a speech. She talked about Martin Luther King Jr. and how, when he gave his final speech, he had no idea how his legacy would live on. She said that he would be proud of her, a little Negro girl from Mississippi, who now had a platform on which to provide entertainment that was intentional, spiritual, and filled with love. It was truly inspiring. She made the moment of the network's launch feel historic, and I was proud to be part of it. TVs around the room were tuned in to the New York countdown of the New Year and the launch of the network. At midnight, there were cheers and kisses all around.

Out of the corner of my eye, I was watching my father. As soon as Oprah sat down next to him, I saw a shift in his attitude. Maybe it was her speech that had affected him, but he seemed to realize the significance of the dinner and the power of this moment. Now Oprah and my father were getting on like a house on fire. He was teasing her. She was laughing. They danced together. He was saying, "Where have you been all my life?" To Oprah!

Meanwhile, Oprah took an intense interest in Redmond. She asked him where he went to school.

"Prison," Redmond said. She asked him where he'd grown up.

"Betty Ford," he said. At some point in the middle of this deep conversation, Redmond stopped to place a call to someone on his cell. I was pretty sure Oprah hadn't had that happen to her in a long time, if ever. But she seemed to respond to the unfiltered young man in front of her.

Oprah asked, "Did you find God in prison?"

Redmond said, "No, I found Satan in prison." It was true that he had come across Satanism in one of his institutional experiences. But then he showed Oprah the Saint Christopher medal he had around his neck and told her that he had grabbed it from our father to wear that night.

Oprah said, "It looks like you found God after all."

Redmond said, "Yes. I found God just now in my dad's car." Oprah had overheard my dad talking gruffly to Redmond. But now Red was holding his own and being honest with her. I wanted so much for my brother. If anyone could change the course of a person's life, a young man who had lost his mother, it would be Oprah.

Now it was close to midnight. Oprah and I stood next to each other, smiling for some photos. After the flashes went off, she turned to face me. She said, "2011 is going to be your year. I swear to you. I'm so proud of you." There I was, in the presence of one of the most spiritually powerful people in the world. She had me by the arm and was telling me that I could help people with my story. I started crying. After four or five hours with the Oprah people, it was all love, giving, understanding, growing, and changing the world.

I felt honored to be part of OWN and all that Oprah was doing. It made me see my time at the beach house in a new light. My eyes were open wider than ever before to the road ahead of me. I saw that my reconnection with Ryan was about more than forgiveness. It was about something bigger. It was letting go of my own past and being grateful for what I had. It was about family, and love, and the ties that bind us forever.

We rang in the New Year. Everyone had a sparkly hat on their head. I put a strand of fake gold pearls around Steadman's neck and said, "You need to be wearing these." There was laughing and hugging. My father was dancing. Things were really looking up.

After midnight, all the guests began to leave. It had been a long night. We came out of the elevator, and Ryan turned to Redmond for the valet ticket. Redmond couldn't find it. Ryan wondered how Redmond could have lost the ticket.

Somehow we managed to convince the valet to give us Ryan's car without the ticket. We crowded into the Porsche, Marketa with a huge gold balloon that bobbled around like an extra head in the car. This was my family! (Well, all except the gold balloon.)

Five minutes later, I was home. My dad said, "Pretty good night, guys. Good job, Tatum." He was proud; I could tell.

First thing in the morning I went to a meeting with my friend Tony. My father texted me: "Guess who had the valet ticket? I had the ticket. Stupid Ryan."

CHAPTER TWENTY-FIVE

CHRISTMAS RAIN DATE

RIGHT AFTER THE New Year, I was planning to move into a new house. Pickle, Wally, my stuff, and I were heading to a four-bedroom Spanish colonial in the Pacific Palisades, right near where my grandparents used to live—and me, too. The house was about a five-minute drive from the beach house. Ryan had joked about that on New Year's Eve, saying, "I'm going to ask my analyst why, if Tatum hates me so much, she is moving so close to me." It was a big house and a nice change. I was excited. And the best feature of the house was that it was on Haverford Street, right down the road from one of the best AA meetings in all of Los Angeles.

Before I moved, there was one last moment I wanted to have at my apartment. Kevin and I were finally going to have a belated Christmas celebration together.

I went down to the lobby to meet him. I grabbed him, held him, and didn't let him go for a good long time. Kevin had never been to this apartment before—I had been to New York to see him, but he hadn't been to L.A. to see me—so I was glad to be able to show it to him, this place that had been so important to me. As soon as he walked in, he said, "I love it. It's just where I'd imagine you living. It has all your stuff, all your smells. My mama."

In the living room, Kevin sank into a chair and stretched. He had been in Carmel with his girlfriend, and it had taken seven hours to drive to my place.

We sipped ginger ale, and I gave Kevin the few presents I hadn't sent to his New York apartment. A fountain pen and a notebook. Some socks. I told him about getting sick, ending up at my dad's, and how it had gone downhill from there. I also talked about gratitude. He'd made it to see me. Here we were. That was what was important.

Kevin asked me to visit New York. He told me that he felt my absence and wanted me to come back more frequently. This was the first time Kevin had mentioned how my departure from New York had affected him. I looked at his long body, stretched out full in the chair. I was so proud of him. He was working while he attended grad school; he was writing a novel; he had a wonderful relationship with his girlfriend. But he still needed me. Had I lost track of Kevin by moving across the country? Kevin was my oldest, my first child. When he was born, I was so in love with him I'd stare and stare and stare at this perfect baby in his crib.

It was with Kevin that I had begun the process of defining myself as a mother and finding my way as a parent. Given the trouble my parents and I had, I knew I wanted to do things different, but that's easy to say. Only on the job did I really figure out what I meant. There were several particular moments I remember as setting me on the path I eventually carved. The first was when Kevin was four, and he had a tooth abscess. We were on the road—in Cincinnati? or was it Toronto?—and the dentist told us the tooth needed to be extracted. When we entered the dentist's office, Kevin was wearing a makeshift cape and carrying a spatula for a sword. Before I knew it they were telling me, "We're taking him in . . . We gotta get this tooth out." Kevin resisted, and they wrapped him in a straitjacket (truly—it was barbaric), while he cried, "Mom, Mom, you can't let them take me away."

I was beside myself. My son had come into the dentist's office a warrior. Adults had reduced him from his powerful self to a crying little child. I had been a wild child—I used to hit the dentist—but Kevin was my golden boy. How could this happen to him? The world seemed so cruel. It was clear to me that I had to put my own emotions aside. My job was to negotiate on his behalf, to get him the medical treatment he needed, of course, but also to make sure he was treated with dignity throughout the process.

Two years later, we found ourselves in the doctor's office. Again, we were on the road, this time in Hawaii for the Davis Cup. Kevin was gravely ill. His intestines were cramping and he had blood in his urine. Red bruising emerged from under his skin. He was in terrible pain. In the island hospital they took an X-ray and found that his spleen was enlarged. They thought he might have leukemia. John was playing a tournament and didn't realize the seriousness of the situation.

Getting Kevin back to New York was scary and horrible. In Children's Hospital my little kindergartner had to undergo several blood tests. John and I handled the situation differently, and it reminded me that in my youth I had experienced a father's inability to handle sickness, trauma—that kind of thing. Suddenly, I saw what I wanted Kevin's experience to be. I didn't want him to see me upset or scared, even when I was. I didn't want him to feel as if he'd done anything wrong, or that he was a burden. I wanted him to feel safe, reassured, and confident that whatever had to be done, I would take care of it and him. It was an approach that hadn't been modeled for me, so I was winging it. When he cried and screamed during blood tests, I focused on calming him down. I was there for him. He would be fine, and we would make it through anything together. It was that simple, but for me it was a turning point as a parent. I made sure my children always knew they were safe, that their feelings mattered, and that I was their advocate.

It turned out that Kevin had an inflammation of the blood vessels called Henoch-Schönlein purpura, an immune reaction triggered by an infection. There were some serious potential side effects, but he came through it like a little warrior.

The second thing I started to do—in between and in spite of having my own problems—was to try to give my children unconditional love. This was in direct response to how my mother handled the issue of her alcoholism with me. My mother lived in the trauma of losing her own parents. She denied the drinking, even when we both knew it was happening. On top of feeling sad and upset that my mother was altered, I was frustrated that she wasn't honest with me. My mother didn't have an addict as a parent, so she didn't know what it felt like. I did, and I didn't want my children's experiences to replicate mine. I told them that if they ever had the sense that something was wrong and believed I had been drinking, they should trust their instincts. It was important to me that my kids feel empowered.

Their feelings were legitimate. I was honest. They knew how hard I was trying, and they could trust that it would take time, but ultimately I would be sober for them.

I brought the good and the bad of my life to my children and hoped they could learn from both. They could learn what to do and what not to do. When I look at all three of my children, I feel like it is working. They call me. They include me in their lives. We have a loving rapport. I've done something very right.

My children and I comprised a small family, and I had no husband or boyfriend. I gave a lot of attention to my children, sometimes too much. But as Kevin and I talked, I realized that leaving the East Coast had changed things for Kevin; I was less available to him, less present in his life. Then and there, I decided that I wouldn't sell my apartment in New York while Kevin was there, not unless I absolutely had to.

I told Kevin, "No mother could be prouder of a child than I am of you. I don't know what I did or didn't do, or if I'm at all responsible for anything you've accomplished, but to know you is a gift and to say I'm your mother is the proudest thing I can say in my life. Good job, Kevin."

Kevin said, "You're my mama. I turned out as well as I have because of you. It's all you, Mom." I sometimes need to hear that.

Before he left, I asked Kevin to use his new fountain pen to write me a note. I handed him a yellow pad. At the top he put the date, and it was just a funny series of vertical lines: "1/1/11." Then he wrote, "Dear Mama, I love you and I need you and I'm here for you forever. Kevin." How lucky am I?

I escorted Kevin downstairs, showing him the building's old elevator from the twenties, which Charlie Chaplin had once ridden. Then Pickle and I sat with him and his little terrier, Nate, in the rental car for a minute. I just wanted to be with him for one more moment. I hate good-byes. The visit had been far too short. I resolved to get to New York more often.

THE NEXT DAY I moved to the new house. This big house on a quiet street was a real life-change. The first night I slept in my room, I was a little haunted by the curtainless windows. It was eerily silent without the West Hollywood traffic. But Pickle kept me warm.

That night I got a good night's sleep and dreamed about riding off into the sunset with a famous Hollywood movie star.

SEAN WAS STILL in Arkansas, where he'd spent Christmas. When he came home, we met for coffee at Greenblatt's on Crescent Heights, my favorite deli. I gave him his Christmas presents, and we talked.

For a while, at least, 2011 was going to be a challenge for me and Sean. I understood the comfort Sean found in coming back to his mother during a challenging time, but we had to be careful about how far we let it go. I didn't want the desire I had to make up for lost time and the guilt at the core of it to influence my parenting. He had a key to my apartment. I was cooking for him several nights a week, which was fine. But I was also doing his laundry, paying his bills, and paying for his acting and singing classes. I paid his rent. I let it go when he said he didn't want to work. My devotion to him wasn't helping him start a career. It was making him less ambitious. I realized I had to pull back a bit.

I was determined to parent him properly going forward. I wanted him to have a work ethic, whatever that meant. I needed to be a mother who told him, "You must step out into the world and give it a try." I can't guilt-trip my kid into doing something. That's not my parenting style. But now, for once, his father and I agreed on what Sean needed. I had to stop supporting him.

It was time for the gravy train to end. If he needed help to deal with his childhood, I would pay for a therapist. He could join a program (Al-Anon) to help children of people with addictions. But we both needed to separate my problems from his growth as a man. My health was not an excuse for postponing the steps he had to make to build a grown-up life. No matter what I'd put him through, it was time for me to set some parental boundaries with Sean.

At Greenblatt's, I told Sean he needed to get a job. He looked at me with his big blue Irish eyes and said, "I'm always working, Mom. I'm an artist." True, he wasn't lazy. But that argument only went so far. I told him that he had to start supporting himself. He reluctantly agreed. It was tough love, and we were at a crossroads, but I was ready and so was he.

SEEING MY SONS inspired me to bring some of what we'd built together to my reconciliation with my father. I vowed to focus on the bigger picture. Taking the high road of unconditional love and support came easily to me as a parent. I needed to find the same road as a daughter. I'd spent two weeks at the beach house. I'd come home, and now I was in my own new, huge, empty house. I felt energized and reborn by the shining new year and ready to have my best year ever.

FOUND

RYAN AND I had arranged to start joint therapy soon after the New Year. It would be the two of us in a room with two therapists, one who was "his" and one who was "mine." I was apprehensive. I heard from Greg that Ryan was nervous, too, and my father sent me a text saying, "Please be nice to me Tatum."

I didn't respond to my dad's text—not because I was planning on being mean!—but because I didn't know exactly what to say. I wanted to be tough and hold true to myself. My only plan was to try to have a conversation without letting his fear of the past override my need for open, honest communication.

Then, unexpectedly, my dear friend Perry died of an overdose in New York. I dropped everything and headed east for the funeral.

From the airport, I took a cab to Kyle's place. Kyle greeted me warmly. His hair, which changes frequently, was short and dark, a handsome contrast to his blue eyes. He was buff as ever, nattily dressed in tight pants and a leather jacket.

Kyle has a beautiful duplex in SoHo, which he shares with his boyfriend, Tim, whom I also love. The first time I returned to New York, I stayed in the spare room, and now it was starting to feel like my home away from home.

As darkness fell, we ordered massive quantities of Chinese food and ate it as we caught up. Kyle was taking a writing class. He let me read some of his work. Afterward, Kyle sat on the floor and listened to me talk about the show and that I felt good about it and about myself. I told him that working on a docuseries was much harder than shooting scripted material. I was used to escaping into a character. Being myself constantly, always miked, without any escape, was mentally exhausting, especially the testimonials, where I sat alone with the cameraman, reflecting on what had just happened. I was constantly delving into my personal life, and not just the life I had chosen and made for myself, but parts of my past that I lived and know about, but, frankly, have chosen not to think about so often anymore. After I wrote *A Paper Life,* I tried to let it all go. Dredging it up again was taking its toll on me as well as on my father. We just handled it in very different ways. But right now Kyle and Chinese food were doing a good job of restoring my soul.

When we ran out of Chinese food, Kyle went to the corner store to buy us cookies, and we ate them as we watched *The Real House-wives of Beverly Hills.* He reflected on how different I was from the Beverly Hills housewives in his beloved reality shows. I had no showy jewels, no gowns, no hair extensions. Kyle thought it was nice that I presented a different model for an age group of women that is too often portrayed as desperately wanting to be younger.

The next day was the funeral, a sad, painful affair. That night, back at Kyle's apartment, my father called to see how I was. It felt good to lean on him during a time of grief. It wasn't a long conversation. My father is a man of brevity. But we were talking like father and daughter, and it didn't feel awkward or clunky. I saw hope in the future. I felt in my gut that things were going to be okay. We'd made some ground. Before we said good-bye, we talked about going to an Academy Awards party together. Through my sadness at losing Perry, I felt the solid, happy heartbeat of my life back in L.A.

I didn't know where we would end up. I have grown and changed so much over the years. I came into this wanting him to understand my experience. I wanted to help him see our history. I thought I could help him. Now, at last, long after it was probably clear to everyone else around us, I finally realized that might never happen, and that it wasn't my responsibility to make it happen. It was that simple.

I didn't know where we would go from here. I couldn't think that far ahead. But we were both trying, and that in itself was a miracle.

I WENT HOME. Pickle greeted me at the door with such unbridled enthusiasm that I decided to take him on a walk. The new house was right near Temescal Canyon Loop, a beautiful four-mile hike in the Santa Monica mountains. Pickle and I strolled through the neighborhood toward the entrance to the trail. As we passed houses, I imagined the lives they contained. A mother making herself coffee. A grandfather checking his e-mail. Women, men, families, children—all those separate, beautiful lives forming delicate paths that wind up and down, crossing one another in familiar and unexpected junctures. Normal people leading an infinite range of lives. I thought about what theirs might be, and how I might want mine to be.

My father and I were truly working to have a relationship. I had come to a place I didn't know I'd ever be. I valued what I had. I didn't have my father for many years. I was past that. I had him now, as much as I needed him or wanted him. This was what he continued to tell me in all the ways he knew how.

We soon reached the trail. Along it, true to L.A.'s reputation, strode many exceptionally fit, healthy people. As we walked, we passed a little park off the trail, where there was a wedding in progress. The sun was shining through the trees. I could see that it was a nice family, giddy with the spirit of the day. A beautiful place for a wedding. A beautiful day. It was inspiring to glimpse the beginning of a life.

After walking for about an hour, Pickle stopped short in the middle of the trail. He was done. I could see I wasn't going to convince him to go any farther, so we turned around and headed home.

BACK AT THE HOUSE, I watched the sunset from my bedroom. It was stunning. I thought about how bright this house would be in the summer, with the sunlight streaming through all its windows. There were four bedrooms—enough room for me and all of my children. There was a backyard for Pickle. When I moved in, I hadn't thought of this place as permanent. But after that walk, I saw how the calm beauty of nature washed over me, even in the midst of the revelations I'd been having. Being in the mountains brought me a peace that overrode even the toughest emotions. I started thinking about what it would be like to stay here for a while. I felt the urge to put down roots, to stay—maybe for several years—in a place where I could take walks and feel close to the sea. Come spring, I could plant some flowers in the garden. I could make a home for myself. If things continued on this path with my dad, in the future, if he needed help or company, I could be closer to him. It was nice to think about settling somewhere. A pleasant feeling surged through me and I smiled as I recognized it. Hope.

I STRUGGLED OVER whether to write this book, casting yet another spotlight on the troubled, messy ups and downs of my efforts to find peace with my father. Was I doing the right thing? Was it another betrayal? Would he see it as such? Could I get in trouble? Would I ruin our chances at reconciliation? I turned to my elder son, Kevin, who is a writer and wise about such things. He said, "Yes, write it, Mama." He told me, simply, that my struggle was part of the whole story.

I came up with the title for this book before I'd finished writing it. I was beginning the process of coming home to Los Angeles and going home to Ryan. I thought that Ryan and I would find each other, and that we would both discover the comfort of being *found*. But every journey is full of question marks. In Ryan's beach house— the place where I had spent most of my childhood—I realized that this home was not the best place for me right now. Life changes. This could change, too.

Journeys don't really end. Even when you reach a destination, the lessons learned are like organisms, stretching and evolving in ways you could never anticipate. When I came to L.A., I didn't feel whole. I thought my father was the missing piece. In some ways, he was. My father and I are not what we could have been, what I'd hoped we'd be. But, corny as it may sound, I found me. My reasons for living, my weaknesses and strengths, my hopes for the future. Knowing myself—*that* is fulfilling. *That* makes me whole.

When I was little, I was a little troublemaker. A feisty, provocative schemer. That part of me is gone. I don't spend much time thinking about that little girl, but I've sometimes wondered what she wanted and what became of her. I turned into someone who'd been scolded once too often. Sometimes I felt like I was missing an outer shield, a thick layer of skin to protect me from the piercing outside air. I was the sensitive pink underbelly. Life was too intense for me. Growing up, being famous confused me—I had external success and it took me a while to feel comfortable admitting that it wasn't enough, because it didn't bring meaningful inner happiness. I dealt with my inner struggles and protected my raw vulnerability by hiding behind a mask of suppression and determination. The layers of protection are so much a part of me that I don't think of stripping them away, but little by little I feel like I am less defined by the world around me and more confident in who I am at my core.

I worry less now about the people around me. My father, my brothers, the people I grew up with, the new friends I've made. I don't need to succeed on their terms. I'm okay, with or without them. They don't make me *me*. I'm my own person. I'm a fighter and will continue to fight. I am proud of myself and my accomplishments.

My journey continues. I think of my brother Griffin. Our lives are forever bound together, and in reconnecting with Ryan I opened up a wound for Griffin, ripping off the scab that may have been on its way toward being healed. I hope and pray that the show doesn't make things worse for him. That is the last thing I want. I still wish that we could all be a family and that my brother and father could resolve their differences. The show is called *The O'Neals: Ryan and Tatum,* and Griffin, whether or not he is on-camera, is an O'Neal, too. I want him to know I see him as part of our family, always, no matter what.

As my children begin their own journeys, my pride carries me alongside them. I come from no schooling, no parenting, no nothin'. I have no idea when Columbus landed. I missed the explanation of how north, south, east, and west work. I don't understand math at all. Algebra? No idea. My children have already learned and achieved more than I ever could have imagined. They have overcome a lot. They are survivors, like me, and they are thriving. Like any parent, I want the best for them, and more than anything, I want us to stay as close as we are today. Forever, if possible.

NO ONE IS a perfect parent, and forgiving my own imperfections means forgiving Ryan his.

There are reasons for Ryan and me to find a way to get along. He is happy having me around. For my part, I see that having a careful, cautious relationship with a difficult parent can be better than having no relationship at all. There is much I still have to heal, and Ryan could help, if he so chooses.

For a time, Ryan and I had the funniest, best relationship that a father and daughter can have. That is preserved on the silver screen forever. Now we have something more nuanced and complex, but just as beautiful.

I was first to try to reconcile with Ryan. I held out an olive branch, asked for some forgiveness, and chose to forgive. It was a challenge for me, and I know it was a challenge for my father, too. Ryan told me, "I hadn't seen you for twenty-five years. You reappeared at Farrah's funeral. You looked wonderful. But I felt like I hardly knew you. I was suspicious. I was torn. I'm less torn now."

I can't exactly say we came to a shared truth, but we forged some inroads. Both of us, in our ways, really tried. Ultimately, in spite of those inroads, I don't think Ryan changed very much in the course of my writing this book. I have learned so much, and I wanted my father to have some of the same revelations I had. I wanted to help him, but I realized that Ryan may not want for himself what I want for him. He, like so many people, may be most comfortable with the status quo. He may never change. Forgiveness, I learned, isn't just about helping, understanding, or changing. A lot of it is just plain acceptance. And I learned that as much as I *want* to help Ryan, I don't *need* to help him. I can only work to improve myself, and that is what I plan to keep doing.

I still hope that Ryan learns that his truths won't kill him. I hope he finds a way to forgive himself for his failures and break the cycle of dealing with his pain through rage and denial. It would be an amazing thing for us to speak openly. There is still so much that we just don't talk about. He has a chance for peace, and, although I'm not going to hold my breath waiting, I'd still do anything to help him find it. Whatever happens from here on, I will live my life without regret. Let's see what happens.

Children are wired to love their parents, and I think I will give my father as many chances as I can, as long as we both live. My father is kinder now. He's more aware of my feelings and sensitive to my needs. As he puts it, "We'll soldier on and pray we keep our dignity." He and I may never see eye to eye, but I hope to keep him in my life.

No doubt we will have ups and downs over the years. We may never reconcile our memories of the past. We will certainly struggle in the present. And the future is still a mystery. I can live with that. What I know for certain is that I tried my hardest, I'm a very courageous survivor, and I'm still out there trying.

LIFE IS FULL of loose ends. For all the time and thought I have given my father, I can't help thinking of the mother I lost, even while she was still alive.

My mother died in Palm Springs in 1997, the week before Thanksgiving. She had three DUIs the year she died. As I got older and looked back at my mother, it was much easier to see the woman she might have been. She had a big laugh. She called everyone Honey Bunny or Snicklefritz or Pumpkin Doodle. Her heart was as big as the state of Georgia. I choose to think of my mother in a loving way. I have enough conflicts in my life. And I feel horrible for any time I didn't treat my mother with the respect that she deserved. My mother never intentionally hurt me. She was so sorry about her failings. She was easy to forgive. When I found out she was dying, I managed to tell her, "I'm sorry, I'm sorry," but it wasn't enough. I wish I could go back as the woman I am today with the time to mend our fractured relationship. I just wish she were still here. I miss her terribly.

There are many questions I never got to ask my mother. She was such a flurry of cigarettes, coffee, and white wine. It was impossible to get her to sit down, slow down, and tell me anything about her life and her roots. Much as my children only know the McEnroe side of their family, I only ever knew the O'Neal side of mine. Someday I hope to find out more about the family I've never known.

My mother lost her parents when she was six. I lost my mother when I was six. And my children lost me for a while there, too. That's three generations of loss and abandonment, and it is my hope that the buck stops with me. If that is my only legacy, I will be proud.

Repairing the trauma of my childhood is a lifelong process. It really has been two steps forward and one step back. But I am still trudging the road of happy destiny. If you look at my path, I am always moving upward and onward, and my life has gotten better, one day at a time. I have never been happier than I am today, and I am waiting eagerly to see what the future holds for me and my children.

When I came back to L.A., I thought I was returning to old friends. Then the move became much more about reconciling with my father and building my career. Now I find myself turning to the physical world of L.A., the solace and joy there is in space, air, sun, and mountains.

The greatest dreams I have are within reach. I dream of one day having Christmas with my whole family: my children, Griffin and his kids, my brother Patrick and his kids, Redmond, my uncle Kevin, and my father. After a lifetime of separation—my God, how great would that be.

I know there must be a reason I have this particular life, and I am grateful for all that it has given me. I am truly blessed.

ACKNOWLEDGMENTS

I WANT TO thank the following people who are my allies, my guides, and my friends: My dad, because he's shown me through this journey that he is a courageous parent and a wonderful father. Jodi Peikoff, whose love and support has been unwavering, and everyone in her office. Ron Castellano, the hardest-working man in the world and the most reliable. Kyle White, whose hair color makes me want to sing into the clouds. I love you, Kyle. Patty Baret, whose words of wisdom and experience, strength and hope, I rely on every day. Pickle O'Neal, whose crazy energy keeps me warm at night and keeps me smiling all day. I love that dog. Birnie Francis, who has stuck with me for thirty years. I love you, old man!! Oprah Winfrey, because she is Oprah and has helped me and millions of women believe even when we didn't. I would like to thank all the wonderful people from the OWN network: Lisa Espramer and Rod Aissa. David Goldberg for taking a chance on us! Greg Johnston, who is an O'Neal at this point. Gilda Brasch, who is right beside Greg in the O'Neal DNA pool. Griffin, Redmond, and Patrick O'Neal, my three brothers whom I love dearly now and forever. My uncle Kevin O'Neal. Andie O'Neal, Joanna O'Neal, Rennon O'Neal, Dillan O'Neal, Damie Deil. All my extended family, whom I don't know now but hope to know one day. And Garrett O'Neal, whom I love and miss. Anjelica Huston for teaching me class, style, and taste. Denis Leary, who has supported me through my ups and downs. Gary Mantoosh, whose spirit and enthusiasm keep me smiling every day. Jen Brehl, another fierce woman advocate and my inspired editor. Hilary Liftin, because she is totally awesome and without her you wouldn't be reading this right now. Hunter Hill, because you are my hero! Rob Parr, who has been dedicated to my physicality for more than twenty-five years. Tracy Cunningham, my L.A.-based hair genius. Steven and Stuart, you know who you are and I love you! Carrie White, you bring light to any room you enter. Sandy Bell, who taught me to let go of the rope. Alexa Lynette, who keeps my bookkeeping in perfect order.

I also am grateful to and want to thank the following people: David Kuhn, Angela Cheng Caplan, Dawn Andrews, Douglas Friedman, Johnny Stuntz (aka Johnny Kat), Mela Murphy, Paul Thomas, Lesley Morrison, Esmé Evans, Sue Mengers, Barry Fox, Shari Sedlis, and Caroline Copley. Ines Taylor, for devoting so much of her life to me and my children. The crew of *The O'Neals*. Wallis, my cat, for being part of my family for seventeen years and now for keeping my dad warm at night. Fariba, hands and feet, always so sweet. Maura Egan, class, grace, and beauty.